The Devil's Dictionaries

(Second Edition)

The Best of

The Devil's Dictionary

by

Ambrose Bierce

&

The American Heretic's Dictionary

(Revised & Expanded)

by

Chaz Bufe

Illustrated by J.R Swanson

See Sharp Press ᵤ Tucson, Arizona ᵤ 2004

For information contact See Sharp Press, P.O. Box 1731,
Tucson, AZ 85702-1731 or go to our web site:
http://www.seesharppress.com

First edition
    First printing—October 1995
    Second printing—May 1997
Second edition
    First printing—September 2004

Bierce, Ambrose, 1842-1914?
    [Devil's Dictionary]
    The Devil's dictionaries : the best of The Devil's dictionary
and The American Heretic's dictionary / by Ambrose Bierce and Chaz
Bufe -- Rev. ed. -- Tucson, AZ : See Sharp Press, 2004.
    186 p. : ill. ; 23 cm.
    ISBN 1-884365-35-3
    1. Satire, American. 2. Capitalism - Humor. 3. Christianity -
Humor. 4. Political science - Humor. I. Title. II. Bufe, Charles.
American heretic's dictionary. III. Title. American heretic's dictionary.
            817.4

Cover design and graphic by Clifford Harper. Interior design by Chaz
Bufe. Interior illustrations by J.R. Swanson.

"All in all, nothing human is worth taking very seriously; nevertheless . . ."

—PLATO

"Sacred cows make the best hamburger."

—ABBIE HOFFMAN

Contents

Introduction

by Earl Lee

Satire is a strange literary form, which seems to have sprung up accidentally, like the red-headed stepchild of comedy. While comedy has had a wide audience and has always been popular in its many forms—including slapstick, puns, limericks, and stand-up—the more intellectual form of satire has traditionally been viewed with suspicion. One suspects that this is so because satire is a political weapon and a social corrective—a strong dose of castor oil for the body politic.

Satire began with the ancient Greeks. Its main forum was the theater, and particularly comedies such as those of Aristophanes. However, as a distinct literary form, satire really began in ancient Rome. There were several great masters of satirical verse, including Persius and Horace. In their poems, the thrust of the "satire" was to gently prod the reader into a more virtuous way of life. As with Ben Franklin's *Poor Richard's Almanack*, the focus was on self-improvement, especially in the areas of frugality, honesty and happiness, and the tactic was gentle criticism. The satires of Horace, for example, have more in common with television series like "Father Knows Best" or "Little House on the Prairie" than with the invective that we today associate with satire.

There were exceptions. In particular, the poet Juvenal was less concerned with improving human behavior, and more concerned with directly attacking those he felt were immoral (in terms of Roman cultural virtues). Juvenal went after hypocrisy, corruption and injustice with a barbed wit that we would associate today with stand-up comedians. He also was ready to attack those he thought were acting foolishly. For example:

Postumus, are you taking a wife?
You used to be sane, what's got into you?
Why endure her nagging when there's a rope
And a window handy, or bridges enough nearby?

(This verse immediately brings to mind Ambrose Bierce's offer to provide a rope or loan a sharp knife to anyone who wanted to commit suicide—they only had to come by his newspaper office and ask. Bierce in fact often used his newspaper column to congratulate successful suicides or to disparage those who had attempted suicide and failed.)

Juvenal's attack-style satires inspired many imitators, and his verse satires were very popular among the Romans. This literary tradition continued in Western literature, and especially in "The Age of Reason" in the 18th century. In English literature, for example, we have Alexander Pope, who perfected verse satire in "The Rape of the Lock." A good short example of his barbed wit is his verse, "Epigram Engraved on the Collar of a Dog Which I Gave to His Royal Highness":

I am his Highness' dog at Kew;
Pray tell me, Sir, whose dog are you?

Another good example is this verse attacking a rival poet:

A gold watch found on cinder whore,
Or a good verse on Jemmy Moore,
Proves but what either should conceal,
Not that they're rich, but that they steal.

Similar satiric attacks abound in both Pope's verse and in his published broadsides. Because of his hunchback, he was an easy target for his enemies. But he usually gave as good as he got. For example, one of Pope's enemies claimed, in a broadside, to have found Pope in a popular bordello and to have pulled Pope off of a prostitute. The broadside included an etching of the author, grabbing Pope by the ankle, and pulling him off of a bed where a young woman is trying to cover herself with a sheet. Of course, Pope quickly responded in kind. Pope's rebuttal was published in a broadside in which Pope claimed essentially, "He had to pull me off; the prostitute was his daughter." English satire included both "corrective" satire and the "attack" style, and Alexander Pope was a master at both.

While English satire was generally either the weapon of personal vendettas or partisan politics, in Europe something new and different was brewing. In France, there was growing cynicism toward both the state and the church. There was a groundswell of opposition to the absolute power of a corrupt nobility and the Catholic Church, not to mention the venality of the merchant class. This inspired the growth of republicanism and deism in France, which has been covered in many books; and, in particular, this move toward political and religious liberty was embodied in the writings of Diderot and Voltaire.

Diderot was one of the leading authors involved in writing the *Encyclopedia*—a massive multi-volume work devoted to promoting science, industry, and intellectual freedom (including deism). Voltaire wrote several articles for this work. It is likely that in 1752, when permission to publish the *Encyclopedia* had been withdrawn (which happened periodically), Voltaire had the idea of publishing a pocket-sized *Philosophical Dictionary*.

Voltaire's main concern seems to have been the fact that most people couldn't afford to buy a 12-volume *Encyclopedia*. Voltaire wanted to create a *Philosophical Dictionary* that could be carried around in a pocket and would be priced within the reach of many Frenchmen. While the *Encyclopedia* would serve as the "cannon" against tyranny, the *Dictionary* would be the "pistol." Published in 1764, Voltaire's book was a great success, and it went through many editions.

The subtlety of his attack on religion and especially the Catholic Church is, to some extent, lost on contemporary readers. But Voltaire's attack had to be oblique, since there was a very real possibility of his being arrested. Over the years, Voltaire denied being the author of the *Philosophical Dictionary*. Later, when that claim was no longer tenable, Voltaire claimed to be only one of several authors. In fact, there are definitions by other authors in his dictionary, but the majority of the work is obviously Voltaire's. The caustic nature of his book is shown, for example, in this definition:

Christian: A good-natured, simple fellow; a true lamb of the fold, who, in the innocence of his heart, persuades himself that he firmly believes unbelievable things that his priests have told him to believe, especially those he cannot even imagine. Consequently he is convinced that three x's make fifteen, that God was made man, that he was hanged and rose to life again, that priests cannot lie, and that all who do not believe in priests will be damned without remission.

Taking leave of Europe and jumping more than a century forward, it is almost certain that Voltaire's *Philosophical Dictionary* was the direct inspiration for Ambrose Bierce's *The Devil's Dictionary*. Compare, for example, Bierce's definition of "Christian" with Voltaire's definition:

Christian, n. One who believes that the New Testament is a divinely inspired book admirably suited to the spiritual needs of his neighbor. One who follows the teachings of Christ in so far as they are not inconsistent with a life of sin.

Bierce's definition has shifted the attack from the Catholic priesthood to the Protestant "priesthood of all believers"—meaning the mob of Bible-bangers who dominated American society at the turn of the 20th century, and who still dominate American politics. But Bierce's attack is still focused on religious fraud and hypocrisy.

While Bierce was an immensely popular journalist in the latter part of the 19th century and the first years of the 20th, since his death Bierce has become an acquired taste. He has a small but devoted readership, made up mostly of those who tend to agree with his cynical view of life and his heretical religious ideas. Bierce called himself an iconoclast, but in reality most of his opinions would have fit in well with those of such 18th-century deists as Ben Franklin and Thomas Paine. Although Bierce did not believe in the Judeo-Christian god, his conservative religious upbringing gave him a profound sense of what divine justice should be. And this was Divine Justice of the Vengeful God sort.

Some of his critics claimed that the "A.G." in A.G. Bierce stood for "Almighty God." Given a world without a vengeful God, Bierce often stepped into that role, using his newspaper column—and particularly his *Devil's Dictionary*—as a cudgel to knock the heads of those who offended his delicate sense of justice. The corrupt politician, the venal businessman, the hypocritical evangelist—they all received blasts from the business-end of Bierce's fiery pen. For example, Bierce was a fierce enemy of the Central Pacific Railroad, which dominated the western United States both politically and economically during the late 19th century. In 1884, he wrote, in "A Corporation is a Fiction, the Men are the Facts":

> Swindling corporations are not objects of our animosity; they are facts of our observation. The real facts of the Central Pacific Railroad company, for example, are Stanford, Crocker and Huntington . . . If the corporation is a thief, it is because Stanford, Crocker and Huntington have stolen . . . Three knaves cannot by combining their rascality make themselves honest men.

As an example of its owners' "rascality," the railroad borrowed $75 million from the federal government to build a rail line to California, and then—while it made millions charging "all the traffic will bear"—lobbied Congress to "forgive" the debt. It was largely due to Bierce's fierce attacks, while writing for the Hearst papers in 1896, that this boondoggle was prevented.

After serving in the army during the Civil War, Bierce's natural cynicism became even more pronounced. The idea for his *Devil's Dictionary* first appeared in 1869 in Bierce's "Town Crier" column written for the San Francisco *News Letter*. The idea fermented until 1875, when the first 48 "A" definitions were published as "The Demon's Dictionary." The project languished for several more years until installments of Bierce's vinegary *Devil's Dictionary* began appearing in 1881 in the San Francisco *Wasp*.

• • • • •

To get an idea of Bierce the man, one can look to another great iconoclast, H.L. Mencken, and his article, "Mr. Mencken Presents: Ambrose Bierce," which appeared in *The World* in 1925.

"The reputation of Ambrose Bierce, like that of Edgar Saltus, has always had something occult and artificial about it. He has been hymned in a passionate, voluptuous way by a small band of disciples, and he has been passed over altogether by the great majority of American critics, and no less by the great majority of American readers. Certainly, it would be absurd to say that he is generally read, even by the intelligentsia. Most of his books, in fact, are out of print and almost unobtainable, and there is little evidence that his massive collected works, printed in twelve volumes between 1909 and 1912, have gone into anything even remotely approaching a wide circulation.

"I have a suspicion, indeed, that Bierce did a serious disservice to himself when he put those twelve volumes together. Already an old man at the time, he permitted his nostalgia for his lost youth to get the better of his critical faculty, never powerful at best, and the result was a depressing assemblage of worn-out and flyblown stuff, much of it quite unreadable. If he had boiled the collection down to four volumes, or even to six, it might have got him somewhere, but as it was his good work was lost in a maze of bad and indifferent work. I doubt that any one save the Bierce fanatics aforesaid, has ever ploughed through the whole twelve volumes. They are filled with epigrams against frauds long dead and forgotten, and echoes of old newspaper controversies, and experiments in fiction that belong to a dark and expired age.

"In the midst of all this blather there are some pearls—more accurately, there are two of them. One consists of a series of epigrams called *The Devil's Dictionary*, the other consists of the war stories, commonly called 'Tales of Soldiers and Civilians.' Among the latter are some of the best war stories ever written—things fully worthy to be ranged beside Zola's 'L' Attaque du Moulin,' Kipling's 'The Taking of Lunztungpen,' or Ludwig Thoma's 'Ein barylscher Soldat.' And among the former are some of the most gorgeous witticisms in the English language.

"Bierce, I believe, was the first writer of fiction ever to treat war realistically. He antedated even Zola. It is common to say that he came out of the Civil War with a deep and abiding loathing for slaughter—that he wrote his war stories as a sort of pacifist. But this is certainly not believed by any one who knew him, as I did in his last years. What he got out of his services in the field was not a sentimental horror of it but a cynical delight in it. It appeared to him as a sort of magnificent reductio ad absurdum of all romance. The world viewed war as something heroic, glorious, idealistic. Very well, he would show how sordid and filthy it was—how stupid, savage, and degrading.

"But to say this is not to say that he disapproved of it. On the contrary, he vastly enjoyed the chance it gave him to set forth dramatically what he was always talking about and gloating over: the infinite imbecility of man. There was nothing of the milk of human kindness in old Ambrose; he did not get the nickname of Bitter Bierce for nothing. What delighted him most in this life was the spectacle of human cowardice and folly. He put man, intellectually, somewhere between the sheep and the horned cattle, and as a hero somewhere below the rats. His war stories, even when they deal with the heroic, do not depict soldiers as heroes; they depict them as bewildered fools, doing things without sense, submitting to torture and outrage without resistance, dying at last like hogs in Chicago, the literary capital of the United States.

"So far in this life, indeed, I have encountered no more thoroughgoing cynic than Bierce. His disbelief in Homo sapiens went even further than Mark Twain's; he was quite unable to imagine the heroic, in any ordinary sense. Nor, for that matter, the wise. Man, to him, was the most stupid and ignoble of animals. But at the same time the most amusing. Out of the spectacle of life about him he got an unflagging and Gargantuan joy. The obscene farce of politics delighted him. He was an almost amorous connoisseur of theology and theologians. He howled with mirth whenever he thought of a professor, a doctor, or a husband. His favorites among he contemporaries were such superb zanies as Bryan, Roosevelt and Hearst.

"Another characteristic that marked him, perhaps flowing out of this same cynicism, was his curious taste for the macabre. All of his stories show it. He delighted in hangings, autopsies, dissecting rooms. Death to him was not something repulsive, but a sort of low comedy—the last act of a squalid and rib rocking buffoonery. When, grown old and weary, he made his way to Mexico, marched into the revolution then going on, and had himself shot, there was certainly nothing in the transaction to surprise his acquaintances. The whole thing was typically Biercian. He died happy, one may be sure, if his executioners made a botch of despatching him—if there was a flash of the grotesque at the end.

"I once enjoyed the curious experience of going to a funeral with him. His conversation to and from the crematory was superb—a long series of gruesome but highly amusing witticisms. He had tales to tell of crematories that had caught fire and singed the mourners, of dead bibuli whose mortal remains had exploded, of widows guarding the fires all night to make sure that their dead husbands did not escape.

"The gentleman whose carcass we were burning had been a literary critic. Bierce suggested that his ashes be molded into bullets and shot at publishers, that they be presented to the library of the New York Lodge of Elks, that they be mailed anonymously to Ella Wheeler Wilcox.

"Later on, when he heard that they had been buried in Iowa, he exploded in colossal mirth. The last time I saw him he predicted that the peasants would dig them up and throw them over the State line. On his own writing desk, he once told me, he kept the ashes of a near relative. I suggested idly that the ceremental urn must be a formidable ornament.

"'Urn, hell!' he exclaimed, 'I keep them in a cigar box!'

"There is no adequate life of Bierce, and I doubt it any will ever be written. His daughter has forbidden the publication of his letters, and shows little hospitality, I am told, to volunteer biographers. One of his disciples, George Sterling, has written about him with great insight and affection, and another, Herman George Scheffauer, has greatly extended his fame abroad, especially in Germany. But neither seems disposed to do him in the grand manner, and I know of no one else competent to do so. He liked mystification, and there are whole stretches of his life that are unaccounted for. His end had mystery in it, too. It is assumed that he was killed in Mexico, but no eyewitness has ever come forward, and so the fact, if it is a fact, remains hanging in the air."

• • • • •

During the first half of the 20th century, Bierce was considered one of the "minor" authors in American literature. But with the growth of the anti-war movement in the 1960s and 1970s, Bierce's short fiction—especially his "Occurrence at Owl Creek Bridge" and his other Civil War stories—found a new audience. Bierce—who was always the cynic's cynic—became popular again in the growing cynicism of the 1970s, a cynicism fed by the lies, hypocrisy, and brutality of America's ruling elite during the Viet Nam debacle.

Now, in the 21st century, with rapidly increasing skepticism about America's "overseas adventures" (as foreign wars were once called, euphemistically) in Afghanistan and Iraq, it is time to reconsider Bierce, his antecedents, and his legacy.

Clearly, one of the heirs to Bierce's style and sympathies is Chaz Bufe. Like Bierce, Bufe lived in San Francisco for many years; and, also like Bierce, he was involved in writing and publishing while in "The City" (as San Francisco residents modestly call their home). But unlike Bierce, Bufe wrote and edited for several radical small magazines (notably *Processed World*) rather than the mainstream, corporate press.

While in San Francisco in the mid-1980s, Bufe created See Sharp Press as an outlet for his own acerbic views and for the radical and freethought writings of other kindred spirits. In 1992, Bufe moved to Tucson, Arizona, and slowly built See Sharp Press into an important small press. In addition to publishing books that attack the vapid religiosity of Alcoholics Anonymous and similar groups, Bufe published books promoting SMART Recovery and other non-religious alternatives to AA. He also pursued his interest in music, publishing several instructional and reference music books. And, last but not least, See Sharp Press has become an important publisher of anarchist and other progressive political materials. See Sharp Press's most successful book to date is in fact the rediscovered original, uncensored edition of Upton Sinclair's classic socialist, muckraking novel, *The Jungle*, which was "lost" for nearly a century but for its momentary reappearance as the very poorly designed 1988 Peachtree edition, now long out of print.

As part of See Sharp Press's series of political books and pamphlets, in 1992 Bufe published his *American Heretics Dictionary*, which was inspired by Bierce's *Devil's Dictionary*. Bufe's *Dictionary* received numerous favorable reviews, with, for instance, the *MENSA Bulletin* commenting: "Such bitterness, such negativity, such unbridled humor, wit and sarcasm."

A few years later, Bufe decided to conflate the two books, combining an updated and expanded version of *The American Heretics Dictionary* with the best selections from Bierce's *Devil's Dictionary* to create *The Devil's Dictionaries* (1995). Again, the reviews were favorable, with *Fact Sheet Five* stating: "You'll never be at a loss for a droll definition again. Keep this on your desk for that emergency epigram or nicely worded insult." The new book was well received and sold well enough—selling out two printings—to justify this new, considerably expanded edition.

This new, second edition of *The Devil's Dictionaries* contains well over 500 definitions from Bufe as well as the best 200+ definitions from Bierce. While the two authors' views on some subjects (especially religion) coincide nearly exactly, they diverge markedly on others. Even so, it is often difficult to tell where Bierce leaves off and Bufe begins. Luckily, our newly born 21st century has provided the author with a wealth of inspiration, and, like Ambrose Bierce's writings, this book displays the full, vigorous cynicism that our own Gilded Age deserves.

—Earl Lee

(Earl Lee is the author of the novel, *Drakulya*, the collection of essays, *Libraries in the Age of Mediocrity*, and the parody of the "Left Behind" series, *Kiss My Left Behind*.)

Bibliography

Bierce, Ambrose. *The Ambrose Bierce Satanic Reader*. Compiled and edited by Ernest J. Hopkins. Garden City, NY: Doubleday, 1968.

Bierce, Ambrose. *The Enlarged Devil's Dictionary*. Edited by Ernest J. Hopkins. Garden City, NY: Doubleday, 1967.

Juvenal. *Juvenal and Persius*. Cambridge, MA : Harvard University Press, 1961.

Pope, Alexander. *The Complete Poetical Works of Alexander Pope*. Boston: Houghton Mifflin, 1931.

Sinclair, Upton. *The Jungle: The Uncensored Original Edition*. Tucson, AZ: See Sharp Press, 2003.

Voltaire. *Pocket Theology*. Girard, Kansas: Haldeman-Julius Co., [1926].

Original Preface to
The Devil's Dictionary

The Devil's Dictionary was begun in a weekly paper in 1881, and was continued in a desultory way and at long intervals until 1906. In that year a large part of it was published in covers with the title *The Cynic's Word Book*, a name which the author had not the power to reject nor the happiness to approve. To quote the publishers of the present [1911] work:

"This more reverent title had previously been forced upon him [Bierce] by the religious scruples of the last newspaper in which a part of the work had appeared, with the natural consequence that when it came out in covers the country already had been flooded by its imitators with a score of 'cynic' books—*The Cynic's This*, *The Cynic's That*, and *The Cynic's t'Other*. Most of these books were merely stupid, though some of them added the distinction of silliness. Among them, they brought the word 'cynic' into disfavor so deep that any book bearing it was discredited in advance of publication."

Meantime, too, some of the enterprising humorists of the country had helped themselves to such parts of the work as served their needs, and many of its definitions, anecdotes, phrases and so forth, had become more or less current in popular speech. This explanation is made, not with any pride of priority in trifles, but in simple denial of possible charges of plagiarism, which is no trifle. In merely resuming his own the author hopes to be held guiltless by those to whom the work is addressed—enlightened souls who prefer dry wines to sweet, sense to sentiment, wit to humor, and clean English to slang.

—Ambrose Bierce, 1911

Preface to
The Devil's Dictionaries
(Second Edition)

Nearly two decades ago, while searching the cluttered and dusty shelves of San Francisco's Community Thrift Store, I found an ancient, tattered hardback, a book for which I'd been searching a number of years. It was Ambrose Bierce's *The Devil's Dictionary*. After buying and reading the book, I was puzzled that no capable writer had produced a modern successor to Bierce's *Dictionary*, and that relatively few attempts at sequels had been made by writers of *any* caliber. While there have been a fairly large number of narrowly focused books modeled on *The Devil's Dictionary* (books dealing with office life and terminology, for instance), there have been remarkably few attempts to produce a wide-ranging, modern successor to Bierce's original. In fact, the only other recent attempt of which I'm aware is a mid-1980s work by a neo-Nazi ("Holocaust revisionist"), which was as vile as it was inept, and which is now, fortunately (and apparently permanently), out of print.

So, in 1991/1992 I wrote *The American Heretic's Dictionary*. It was, of course, modeled on Bierce's *Devil's Dictionary*, but differed from it in many respects. For one thing, it was far shorter, containing slightly over 300 definitions in comparison with the approximate 1000 in Bierce's original. However, the *Heretic's Dictionary* benefitted greatly from J.R. Swanson's brilliant, acerbic illustrations, which fleshed it out to a large degree.

Another difference between the *American Heretic's Dictionary* and *The Devil's Dictionary* was that my targets were somewhat different than Bierce's, which is understandable given the near-century between the writing of his book and the writing of mine. While Bierce and I attacked many of the same things—religion, superstition, politicians, journalists, corporations, and hypocrisy in its manifold, multi-colored forms—I was freer than Bierce to deal with topics which were taboo in his time, particularly sex. Conversely, unlike Bierce, I didn't attack racial or ethnic groups, nor did I attack women. Rather, I took pains not to attack those who have little power and who are routinely victimized. Instead, I went after the powerful: big business, government, the military, the police, America's pathetic political parties, the corporate media, and organized religion—institutions that most American "humorists" avoid confronting in an effort to make themselves palatable to the corporate media.

Another notable, though not immediately apparent, difference between my definitions and those of Bierce is in their underlying premises. Bierce was an undying pessimist who believed that human nature is unalterably base, and that there is no hope whatsoever for humanity. In contrast, I consider Bierce's basic premise naive—Bierce was wrong in thinking that "human nature" is fixed; there's good evidence that it is not fixed, but rather is to a great extent the product of environment, and that therefore the human situation only *seems* hopeless.

Three years after *The American Heretic's Dictionary* appeared, I revised a number of its definitions and added approximately 140 new ones. I then decided to juxtapose my definitions with Bierce's best definitions in a new book, *The Devil's Dictionaries* (thus inviting comparisons between the two sets of definitions). At that point I commissioned J.R. Swanson to do several new illustrations and carefully went through Bierce's *Devil's Dictionary* a number of times to select what I considered his best definitions—just over 200, all of which still pack a punch and appeal to modern readers; the rest, I believed, would leave such readers scratching their heads and muttering, "What's funny about *that!?*"

Indeed, many readers will probably read at least one of Bierce's definitions ("Woman") and say precisely that to themselves. I included this definition because Bierce was a notorious misogynist, and I thought it best not to hide the fact. (Bierce's favorite toast was "Here's to woman! Could we but fall into her arms without falling into her hands!"; and he once wrote that the sum contribution of women to the building of civilization amounted to less than the invention of the bicycle.) I also included Bierce's definition of Woman because, though I recognize how obnoxious it is, I still find it rather funny.

I did not, however, include any of Bierce's very few definitions regarding race, because I consider them both weak and distasteful. My primary concern in this book is to entertain, and my secondary concern is to dispel popular delusions; and including those definitions would have served neither purpose.

In the new definitions I wrote for the 1995 edition of *The Devil's Dictionaries*, I added a few that attack the hypocrisies and double standards that women exhibit in their attitudes toward and treatment of men. This seems fair, because they complement definitions which attack men's attitude and behaviors (e.g., "Automobile" and "Penis"); and I heard no complaints about them.

The book sold well enough—and raised enough anguished howls of "That's just *not* funny!"—to prod me to think of producing an expanded, second edition. The selection of George W. Bush as president by The Supremes and the subsequent actions of his "God chosen" administration were all the impetus I needed to begin work on the volume you hold in your hands. Rarely if ever in the history of the republic has there been such a shameless display of venality, arrogance, incompetence, brutality, hypocrisy, and appalling, indeed astounding, stupidity. To put this another way, this new, second edition of *The Devil's Dictionaries* is in large part the result of the never-ending inspiration of the one, the only George W. Bush. (My other sources of inspiration for this new edition were, of course, the ongoing circus of religious fundamentalism, the appalling "reporting" of the corporate "news" media, and the ever-vaster wastelands of television and what passes for popular culture in this country; as one anonymous wit put it, "another day, another outrage"—an epigram which is both politically and culturally apt.)

For this new edition I wrote 90 new definitions, revised (and often expanded) perhaps 150 others, and deleted around 15 that I considered weak or redundant. To illustrate all this, J.R. Swanson produced seven new, pungent drawings. The end result is this second edition containing over 200 of Bierce's definitions, over 500 of mine, and over 50 of J.R.'s illustrations.

Before concluding, I would like to acknowledge and thank all those who were good enough to allow me to use their definitions or whose words inspired me to write definitions. They include, in no particular order, Earl Lee, Albert Ellis, David Irish, John Rush,

Bill Griffith, Vince Fox, Vince Williams, Greg Williamson, Fred Woodworth, Yves Barbero, Oscar Wilde, that most prolific of writers, Anonymous, and, of course, Ambrose Bierce. Many others also provided definitions or inspiration, and I did my best to acknowledge all of them within the text; if I missed anyone, my sincere apologies—it wasn't deliberate.

So, sit back, relax, and enjoy the book—at least until you hit that one inevitable definition that leaves you grinding your teeth and muttering, "that's simply *not funny!*" Neither Bierce nor I would have done our jobs if there wasn't something in *The Devil's Dictionaries* to offend everyone.

—Chaz Bufe

The Best of

The Devil's Dictionary

by

Ambrose Bierce

A

ABNORMAL, adj. Not conforming to standard. In matters of thought and conduct, to be independent is to be abnormal, to be abnormal is to be detested. . . .

ABSTAINER, n. A weak person who yields to the temptation of denying himself a pleasure. . . .

ABSURDITY, n. A statement or belief manifestly inconsistent with one's own opinion.

ACCIDENT, n. An inevitable occurrence due to the action of immutable natural laws.

ADMIRATION, n. Our polite recognition of another's resemblance to ourselves.

ADORE, v. t. To venerate expectantly.

ALDERMAN, n. An ingenious criminal who covers his secret thieving with a pretence of open marauding.

ALLIANCE, n. In international politics, the union of two thieves who have their hands so deeply inserted in each other's pocket that they cannot separately plunder a third.

ALONE, adj. In bad company.

ARENA, n. In politics, an imaginary rat-pit in which the statesman wrestles with his record.

ALTAR, n. The place whereon the priest formerly raveled out the small intestine of the sacrificial victim for purposes of divination and cooked its flesh for the gods. The word is now seldom used, except with reference to the sacrifice of their liberty and peace by a male and a female fool.

APPEAL, v.t. In law, to put the dice into the box for another throw.

B

BENEFACTOR, n. One who makes heavy purchases of ingratitude, without, however, materially affecting the price, which is still within the means of all.

BIGAMY, n. A mistake in taste for which the wisdom of the future will adjudge a punishment called trigamy.

BIRTH, n. The first and direst of all disasters. . . .

BORE, n. A person who talks when you wish him to listen.

BRIDE, n. A woman with a fine prospect of happiness behind her.

BRUTE, n. See "Husband."

C

CABBAGE, n. A familiar kitchen-garden vegetable about as large and wise as a man's head. . . .

CALLOUS, adj. Gifted with great fortitude to bear the evils afflicting another. . . .

CAPITAL, n. The seat of misgovernment. . . .

CHRISTIAN, n. One who believes that the New Testament is a divinely inspired book admirably suited to the spiritual needs of his neighbor. One who follows the teachings of Christ in so far as they are not inconsistent with a life of sin.

CLAIRVOYANT, n. A person, commonly a woman, who has the power of seeing that which is invisible to her patron—namely, that he is a blockhead.

CONSERVATIVE, n. A statesman who is enamored of existing evils, as distinguished from the Liberal, who wishes to replace them with others.

CONSULT, v. t. To seek another's approval of a course already decided on.

CORPORATION, n. An ingenious device for obtaining individual profit without individual responsibility.

CYNIC n. A blackguard whose faulty vision sees things as they are, not as they ought to be. . . .

D

DAWN, n. The time when men of reason go to bed. Certain old men prefer to rise at about that time, taking a cold bath and a long walk with an empty stomach, and otherwise mortifying the flesh. They then point with pride to these practices as the cause of their sturdy health and ripe years; the truth being that they are hearty and old, not because of their habits, but in spite of them. The reason we find only robust persons doing this thing is that it has killed all the others who have tried it.

DAY, n. A period of twenty-four hours, mostly misspent. . . .

DEBT, n. An ingenious substitute for the chain and whip of the slave-driver.

DEFENCELESS, adj. Unable to attack.

DELEGATION, n. In American politics, an article of merchandise that comes in sets.

DELIBERATION, n. The act of examining one's bread to determine which side it is buttered on.

DESTINY, n. A tyrant's authority for crime and a fool's excuse for failure.

Diaphragm, n. A muscular partition separating disorders of the chest from disorders of the bowels.

Diplomacy, n. The patriotic art of lying for one's country.

Discussion, n. A method of confirming others in their errors.

Disobedience, n. The silver lining to the cloud of servitude.

Distance, n. The only thing that the rich are willing for the poor to call theirs, and keep.

Divination, n. The art of nosing out the occult. Divination is of as many kinds as there are fruit-bearing varieties of the flowering dunce and the early fool.

E

Eccentricity, n. A method of distinction so cheap that fools employ it to accentuate their incapacity.

Egotist, n. A person of low taste, more interested in himself than in me.

Epitaph, n. An inscription on a tomb, showing that virtues acquired by death have a retroactive effect. Following is a touching example:

Here lie the bones of Parson Platt,
Wise, pious, humble and all that,
Who showed us life as all should live it;
Let that be said—and God forgive it!

EULOGY, n. Praise of a person who has either the advantages of wealth and power, or the consideration to be dead.

EVANGELIST, n. A bearer of good tidings, particularly (in a religious sense) such as assure us of our own salvation and the damnation of our neighbors.

EVERLASTING, adj. Lasting forever. . . .

EXCEPTION, n. A thing which takes the liberty to differ from other things of its class, as an honest man, a truthful woman, etc. "The exception proves the rule" is an expression constantly upon the lips of the ignorant, who parrot it from one another with never a thought of its absurdity. In the Latin, "Exceptio probat regulam" means that the exception tests the rule, puts it to the proof, not confirms it. The malefactor who drew the meaning from this excellent dictum and substituted a contrary one of his own exerted an evil power which appears to be immortal.

EXILE, n. One who serves his country by residing abroad, yet is not an ambassador.

F

FAITH, n. Belief without evidence in what is told by one who speaks without knowledge, of things without parallel.

FEAST, n. A festival. A religious celebration usually signalized by gluttony and drunkenness, frequently in honor of some holy person distinguished for abstemiousness. . . .

FLAG, n. A colored rag borne above troops and hoisted on forts and ships. It appears to serve the same purpose as certain signs that one sees on vacant lots in London—"Rubbish may be shot here."

FLY-SPECK, n. The prototype of punctuation. It is observed by Garvinus that the systems of punctuation in use by the various literary nations depended originally upon the social habits and general diet of the flies infesting the several countries. These creatures, which have always been distinguished for a neighborly and companionable familiarity with authors, liberally or niggardly embellish the manuscripts in process of growth under the pen, according to their bodily habit, bringing out the sense of the work by a species of interpretation superior to, and independent of, the writer's powers. . . . Fully to understand the important services that flies perform to literature, it is only necessary to lay a page of some popular novelist alongside a saucer of cream-and-molasses in a sunny room and observe "how the wit brightens and the style refines" in accurate proportion to the duration of exposure.

FOREFINGER, n. The finger commonly used in pointing out two malefactors.

FORGETFULNESS, n. A gift of God bestowed upon debtors in compensation for their destitution of conscience.

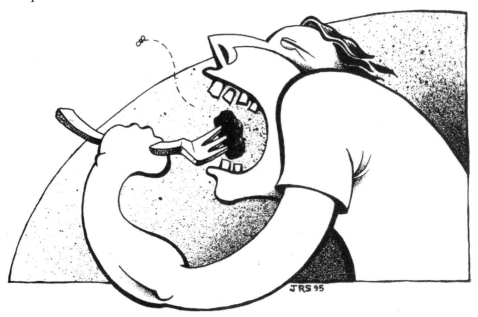

FORK, n. An instrument used chiefly for the purpose of putting dead animals into the mouth. . . .

FREEBOOTER, n. A conqueror in a small way of business, whose annexations lack the sanctifying merit of magnitude.

FREEDOM, n. Exemption from the stress of authority in a beggarly half dozen of restraint's infinite multitude of methods. A political condition that every nation supposes itself to enjoy in virtual monopoly. Liberty. The distinction between freedom and liberty is not accurately known; naturalists have never been able to find a living specimen of either.

FRIENDLESS, n. Having no favors to bestow. Destitute of fortune. Addicted to utterance of truth and common sense.

FRIENDSHIP, n. A ship big enough to carry two in fair weather, but only one in foul.

FUNERAL, n. A pageant whereby we attest our respect for the dead by enriching the undertaker, and strengthen our grief by an expenditure that deepens our groans and doubles our tears.

FUTURE, n. That period of time in which our affairs prosper, our friends are true and our happiness assured.

G

GLUTTON, n. A person who escapes the evils of moderation by committing dyspepsia.

GOUT, n. A physician's name for the rheumatism of a rich patient.

GRAVE, n. A place in which the dead are laid to await the coming of the medical student.

H

HABEAS CORPUS, n. A writ by which a man may be taken out of jail when confined for the wrong crime.

HAG, n. An elderly lady whom you do not happen to like . . .

HAPPINESS, n. An agreeable sensation arising from contemplating the misery of another.

HEARSE, n. Death's baby carriage.

HEATHEN, n. A benighted creature who has the folly to worship something that he can see and feel. . . .

HISTORY, n. An account mostly false, of events mostly unimportant, which are brought about by rulers mostly knaves, and soldiers mostly fools.

IDIOT, n. A member of a large and powerful tribe whose influence in human affairs has always been dominant and controlling. The Idiot's activity is not confined to any special field of thought or action, but "pervades and regulates the whole." He has the last word in everything; his decision is unappealable. He sets the fashions of opinion and taste, dictates the limitations of speech and circumscribes conduct with a dead-line.

I

IMMIGRANT, n. An unenlightened person who thinks one country better than another.

IMMORAL, adj. Inexpedient. . . .

IMPARTIAL, adj. Unable to perceive any promise of personal advantage from espousing either side of a controversy or adopting either of two conflicting opinions.

IMPOSTOR, n. A rival aspirant to public honors.

IMPUNITY, n. Wealth.

INCOMPATIBILITY, n. In matrimony, a similarity of tastes, particularly the taste for domination. Incompatibility may, however, consist of a meek-eyed matron living just around the corner. It has even been known to wear a moustache.

INDIGESTION, n. A disease which the patient and his friends frequently mistake for deep religious conviction and concern for the salvation of mankind. As the simple Red Man of the western wild put it, with, it must be confessed, a certain force: "Plenty well, no pray; big bellyache, heap God."

INEXPEDIENT, adj. Not calculated to advance one's interests.

INFIDEL, n. In New York, one who does not believe in the Christian religion; in Constantinople, one who does. . . .

INK, n. A villainous compound of tanno-gallate of iron, gum arabic and water, chiefly used to facilitate the infection of idiocy and promote intellectual crime. . . .

INSURRECTION, n. An unsuccessful revolution. Disaffection's failure to substitute misrule for bad government.

J

JEALOUS, adj. Unduly concerned about the preservation of that which can be lost only if not worth keeping.

K

KLEPTOMANIAC, n. A rich thief.

KORAN, n. A book which the Mohammedans foolishly believe to have been written by divine inspiration, but which Christians know to be a wicked imposture, contradictory to Holy Scriptures.

L

LABOR, n. One of the processes by which A acquires property for B.

LAND, n. A part of the earth's surface, considered as property. The theory that land is property subject to private ownership and control is the foundation of modern society, and is eminently worthy of the superstructure. Carried to its logical conclusion, it means that some have the right to prevent others from living; for the right to own implies the right exclusively to occupy; and in fact laws of trespass are enacted wherever property in land is recognized. It follows that if the whole area of terra firma is owned by A, B and C, there will be no place for D, E, F and G to be born, or, born as trespassers, to exist.

LAWFUL, adj. Compatible with the will of a judge having jurisdiction.

LAWYER, n. One skilled in circumvention of the law.

LEXICOGRAPHER, n. A pestilent fellow who, under the pretense of recording some particular stage in the development of a language, does what he can to arrest its growth. . . .

LIBERTY, n. One of Imagination's most precious possessions.

LICKSPITTLE, n. A useful functionary, not infrequently found editing a newspaper. . . .

LITIGATION, n. A machine which you go into as a pig and come out of as a sausage.

LOCK-AND-KEY, n. The distinguishing device of civilization and enlightenment.

LOGIC, n. The art of thinking and reasoning in strict accordance with the limitations and incapacities of the human misunderstanding. The basis of logic is the syllogism, consisting of a major and a minor premise and a conclusion—thus:

Major Premise: Sixty men can do a piece of work sixty times as quickly as one man.
Minor Premise: One man can dig a post-hole in sixty seconds; therefore—
Conclusion: Sixty men can dig a post-hole in one second.

This many be called the syllogism arithmetical, in which, by combining logic and mathematics, we obtain a double certainty and are twice blessed.

LONGEVITY, n. Uncommon extension of the fear of death.

LOQUACITY, n. A disorder which renders the sufferer unable to curb his tongue when you wish to talk.

LOVE, n. A temporary insanity curable by marriage or by removal of the patient from the influences under which he incurred the disorder. This disease, like caries and many other ailments, is prevalent only among civilized races living under artificial conditions; barbarous nations breathing pure air and eating simple food enjoy immunity from its ravages. It is sometimes fatal, but more frequently to the physician than to the patient.

M

MACHINATION, n. The method employed by one's opponents in baffling one's open and honorable efforts to do the right thing.

MAGIC, n. The art of converting superstition into coin. There are other arts serving the same high purpose, but the discreet lexicographer does not name them.

MARRIAGE, n. The state or condition of a community consisting of a master, a mistress and two slaves, making in all, two.

MISS, n. A title with which we brand unmarried women to indicate that they are in the market.

MONUMENT, n. A structure intended to commemorate something which either needs no commemoration or cannot be commemorated. . . . The monument custom has its *reductiones ad absurdum* in monuments "to the unknown dead"—that is to say, monuments to perpetuate the memory of those who have left no memory.

N

NEPOTISM, n. Appointing your grandmother to office for the good of the party.

NOSE, n. The extreme outpost of the face. From the circumstance that great conquerors have great noses, Getius, whose writings antedate the age of humor, calls the nose the organ of quell. It has been observed that one's nose is never so happy as when thrust into the affairs of another, from which some physiologists have drawn the inference that the nose is devoid of the sense of smell.

NOVEL, n. A short story padded. . . .

O

OBSOLETE, adj. No longer used by the timid. Said chiefly of words. A word which some lexicographer has marked obsolete is ever thereafter an object of dread and loathing to the fool writer, but if it is a good word and has no exact modern equivalent equally good, it is good enough for the good writer. Indeed, a writer's atti-

attitude toward "obsolete" words is as true a measure of his literary ability as anything except the character of his work. A dictionary of obsolete and obsolescent words would not only be singularly rich in strong and sweet parts of speech; it would add possessions to the vocabulary of every competent writer who might not happen to be a competent reader.

OCCASIONAL, adj. Afflicting us with greater or less frequency. That, however, is not the sense in which the word is used in the phrase "occasional verses," which are verses written for an "occasion," such as an anniversary, a celebration or other event. True, they afflict us a little worse than other sorts of verse, but their name has no reference to irregular occurrence.

OCCIDENT, n. The part of the world lying west (or east) of the Orient. It is largely inhabited by Christians, a powerful subtribe of the Hypocrites, whose principal industries are murder and cheating, which they are pleased to call "war" and "commerce." These, also, are the principal industries of the Orient.

OCEAN, n. A body of water occupying about two-thirds of a world made for man—who has no gills.

OMEN, n. A sign that something will happen if nothing happens.

OPPORTUNITY, n. A favorable occasion for grasping a disappointment.

OPPOSITION, n. In politics the party that prevents the Government from running amuck by hamstringing it. . . .

OPTIMISM, n. The doctrine, or belief, that everything is beautiful, including what is ugly, everything good, especially the bad, and everything right that is wrong. It is held with greatest tenacity by those most accustomed to the mischance of falling into adversity, and is most acceptably expounded with the grin that apes a smile. Being a blind faith, it is inaccessible to the light of disproof—an intellectual disorder, yielding to no treatment but death. It is hereditary, but fortunately not contagious.

OPTIMIST, n. A proponent of the doctrine that black is white.

ORPHAN, n. A living person whom death has deprived of the power of filial ingratitude . . .

ORTHODOX, n. An ox wearing the popular religious yoke.

OUTDO, v.t. To make an enemy.

OUT-OF-DOORS, n. That part of one's environment upon which no government has been able to collect taxes. . . .

OVERWORK, n. A dangerous disorder affecting high public functionaries who want to go fishing.

P

PAINTING, n. The art of protecting flat surfaces from the weather and exposing them to the critic.

Formerly, painting and sculpture were combined in the same work: the ancients painted their statues. The only present alliance between the two arts is that the modern painter chisels his patrons.

PALM, n. A species of tree having several varieties, of which the familiar "itching palm" (*Palma hominis*) is most widely distributed and sedulously cultivated. This noble vegetable exudes a kind of invisible gum, which may be detected by applying to the bark a piece of gold or silver. The metal will adhere with remarkable tenacity. The fruit of the itching palm is so bitter and unsatisfying that a considerable percentage of it is sometimes given away in what are known as "benefactions."

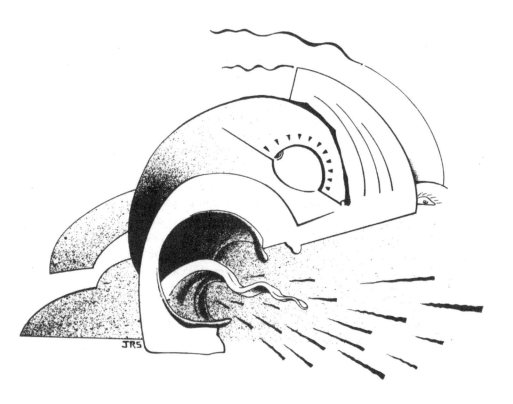

PAIN, n. An uncomfortable frame of mind that may have a physical basis in something that is being done to the body, or may be purely mental, caused by the good fortune of another.

PALMISTRY, n. The 947th method (according to Mimbleshaw's classification) of obtaining money by false pretences. It consists in "reading character" in the wrinkles made by closing the hand. The pretence is not altogether false; character can really be read very accurately in this way, for the wrinkles in every hand submitted plainly spell the word "dupe." The imposture consists in not reading it aloud.

PANTHEISM, n. The doctrine that everything is God, in contradistinction to the doctrine that God is everything.

PARDON, v. To remit a penalty and restore to a life of crime. To add to the lure of crime the temptation of ingratitude.

PASSPORT, n. A document treacherously inflicted upon a citizen going abroad, exposing him as an alien and pointing him out for special reprobation and outrage.

PAST, n. That part of Eternity with some small fraction of which we have a slight and regrettable acquaintance. A moving line called the Present parts it from an imaginary period known as the Future. These two grand divisions of Eternity, of which the one is continually effacing the other, are entirely unlike. The one is dark with sorrow and disappointment, the other bright with prosperity and joy. The Past is the region of sobs, the Future is the realm of song. In the one crouches Memory, clad in sackcloth and ashes, mumbling penitential prayer; in the sunshine of the other Hope flies with a free wing, beckoning to temples of success and bowers of ease. . . .

PASTIME, n. A device for promoting dejection. Gentle exercise for intellectual debility.

PATIENCE, n. A minor form of despair, disguised as a virtue.

PATRIOT, n. One to whom the interests of a part seem superior to those of the whole. The dupe of statesmen and the tool of conquerors.

PATRIOTISM, n. Combustible rubbish ready to the torch of any one ambitious to illuminate his name.
  In Dr. Johnson's famous dictionary patriotism is defined as the last resort of a scoundrel. With all due respect to an enlightened but inferior lexicographer, I beg to submit that it is the first.

PEACE, n. In international affairs, a period of cheating between two periods of fighting.

PERSEVERANCE, n. A lowly virtue whereby mediocrity achieves an inglorious success.

PHILANTHROPIST, n. A rich (and usually bald) old gentleman who has trained himself to grin while his conscience is picking his pocket.

PHILOSOPHY, n. A route of many roads leading from nowhere to nothing.

PIANO, n. A parlor utensil for subduing the impenitent visitor. It is operated by depressing the keys of the machine and the spirits of the audience.

PITIFUL, adj. The state of an enemy or opponent after an imaginary encounter with oneself.

PLAGIARIZE, v. To take the thought or style of another writer whom one has never, never read.

PLATITUDE, n. The fundamental element and special glory of popular literature. A thought that snores in words that smoke. The wisdom of a million fools in the diction of a dullard. A fossil sentiment in artificial rock. A moral without the fable. All that is mortal of a departed truth. A demitasse of milk-and-morality. The Pope's-nose of a featherless peacock. A jelly-fish withering on the shore of the sea of thought. The cackle surviving the egg. A desiccated epigram.

PLUNDER, v. To take the property of another without observing the decent and customary reticences of theft. . . . To wrest the wealth of A from B and leave C lamenting a vanished opportunity.

POLITENESS, n. The most acceptable hypocrisy.

POLITICIAN, n. An eel in the fundamental mud upon which the superstructure of organized society is reared. When he wriggles he mistakes the agitation of his tail for the trembling of the edifice. As compared with the statesman, he suffers the disadvantage of being alive.

Politics, n. A strife of interests masquerading as a contest of principles. The conduct of public affairs for private advantage.

Positive, adj. Mistaken at the top of one's voice.

Pray, v. To ask that the laws of the universe be annulled in behalf of a single petitioner confessedly unworthy.

Preference, n. A sentiment, or frame of mind, induced by the erroneous belief that one thing is better than another. An ancient philosopher, expounding his conviction that life is no better than death, was asked by a disciple why, then, he did not die. "Because," he replied, "death is no better than life."
It is longer.

Prerogative, n. A sovereign's right to do wrong.

Prescription, n. A physician's guess at what will best prolong the situation with least harm to the patient.

Price, n. Value, plus a reasonable sum for the wear and tear of conscience in demanding it.

Proof, n. Evidence having a shade more of plausibility than of unlikelihood. The testimony of two credible witness as opposed to that of only one.

Providential, adj. Unexpectedly and conspicuously beneficial to the person so describing it.

Q

QUILL, n. An implement of torture yielded by a goose and commonly wielded by an ass. . . .

QUOTATION, n. The act of repeating erroneously the words of another. . . .

R

RABBLE, n. In a republic, those who exercise a supreme authority tempered by fraudulent elections. . . .

RACK, n. An argumentative implement formerly much used in persuading devotees of a false faith to embrace the living truth.

RAILROAD, n. The chief of many mechanical devices enabling us to get away from where we are to where we are no better off.

RASH, adj. Insensible to the value of our advice.

REALLY, adv. Apparently.

REASONABLE, adj. Accessible to the infection of our own opinions. Hospitable to persuasion, dissuasion and evasion.

RECONSIDER, v. To seek a justification for a decision already made.

REDRESS, n. Reparation without satisfaction.

REFLECTION, n. An action of the mind whereby we obtain a clearer view of our relation to the things of yesterday and are able to avoid the perils that we shall not again encounter.

RELIGION, n. A daughter of Hope and Fear, explaining to Ignorance the nature of the Unknowable. . . .

REPARTEE, n. Prudent insult in retort. Practiced by gentlemen with a constitutional aversion to violence, but a strong disposition to offend. . . .

REPROBATION, n. In theology, the state of a luckless mortal prenatally damned. The doctrine of reprobation was taught by Calvin, whose joy in it was somewhat marred by the sad sincerity of his conviction that although some are foredoomed to perdition, others are predestined to salvation.

RESIDENT, adj. Unable to leave.

RESOLUTE, adj. Obstinate in a course that we approve.

RESTITUTION, n. The founding or endowing of universities and public libraries by gift or bequest.

REVELATION, n. A famous book in which St. John the Divine concealed all that he knew. . . .

REVERENCE, n. The spiritual attitude of a man to a god and a dog to a man.

REVOLUTION, n. In politics, an abrupt change in the form of mis-government. Specifically, in American history, the substitution of the rule of an Administration for that of a Ministry, whereby the welfare and happiness of the people were advanced a full half-inch. Revolutions are usually accompanied by a considerable effusion of blood, but are accounted worth it—this appraisement being made by beneficiaries whose blood had not the chance to be shed.

RIME, n. Agreeing sounds in the terminals of verse, mostly bad. The verses themselves, as distinguished from prose, mostly dull. Usually (and wickedly) spelled "rhyme."

R.I.P. A careless abbreviation of *requiescat in pace*, attesting to an indolent goodwill to the dead. According to the learned Dr. Drigge, however, the letters originally meant nothing more that *reductus in pulvis*.

ROAD, n. A strip of land along which one may pass from where it is too tiresome to be to where it is futile to go.

RUM, n. Generically, fiery liquors that produce madness in total abstainers.

S

SAINT, n. A dead sinner revised and edited. . . .

SATAN, n. One of the Creator's lamentable mistakes, repented in sashcloth and axes.

Being instated as an archangel, Satan made himself multifariously objectionable and was finally expelled from Heaven. Halfway in his descent he paused, bent his head in thought a a moment and at last went back. "There is one favor that I should like to ask," said he.

"Name it."

"Man, I understand, is about to be created. He will need laws."

"What, wretch! You his appointed adversary, charged from the dawn of eternity with hatred of his soul—you ask for the right to make his laws?"

"Pardon; what I have to ask is that he be permitted to make them himself."

It was so ordered.

SAW, n. A trite popular saying, or proverb. (Figurative and colloquial.) So called because it makes its way into a wooden head. Following are examples of old saws fitted with new teeth.

A penny saved is a penny to squander.
A man is known by the company that he organizes.
A bad workman quarrels with the man who calls him that.
A bird in the hand is worth what it will bring.
Better late that before anybody has invited you.
Example is better than following it.
Half a loaf is better than a whole one if there is much else.
Think twice before you speak to a friend in need.
What is worth doing is worth the trouble of asking somebody to do it.
Least said is soonest disavowed.
He laughs best who laughs least.
Speak of the Devil and he will hear about it.
Of two evils choose to be the least.
Strike while your employer has a big contract.
Where there's a will there's a won't.

SCARIFICATION, n. A form of penance practised by the mediaeval pious. The rite was performed, sometimes with a knife, sometimes with a hot iron, but always, says Arsenius Asceticus, acceptably if the penitent spared himself no pain nor harmless disfigurement. Scarification, with other crude penances, has now been superseded by benefaction. The founding of a library or endowment of a university is said to yield to the penitent a sharper and more lasting pain than is conferred by the knife or iron, and is therefore a surer means of grace. There are, however, two grave objections to it as a penitential method: the good that it does and the taint of justice.

SERIAL, n. A literary work, usually a story that is not true, creeping through several issues of a newspaper or magazine. Frequently appended to each instalment is a "synopsis of preceding chapters" for those who have not read them, but a direr need is a synopsis of succeeding chapters for those who do not intend to read them. A synopsis of the entire work would be still better. . . .

SCRIBBLER, n. A professional writer whose views are antagonistic to one's own.

SCRIPTURES n. The sacred books of our holy religion, as distinguished from the false and profane writings on which all other faiths are based.

SELF-ESTEEM, n. An erroneous appraisement.

SELF-EVIDENT, adj. Evident to one's self and to nobody else.

SLANG, n. The grunt of the human hog (*Pignoramus intolerabilis*) with a audible memory. The speech of one who utters with his tongue what he thinks with his ear, and feels the pride of a creator in accomplishing the feat of a parrot.

SUCCESS, n. The one unpardonable sin against one's fellows.

T

TAKE, v.t. To acquire, frequently by force but preferably by stealth.

TALK, v. To commit an indiscretion without temptation, from an impulse without purpose.

TARIFF, n. A scale of taxes on imports, designed to protect the domestic producer against the greed of his consumer.

TELEPHONE, n. An invention of the devil which abrogates some of the advantages of making a disagreeable person keep his distance.

TENACITY, n. A certain quality of the human hand in its relation to the coin of the realm. It attains its highest development in the hand of authority and is considered a serviceable equipment for a career in politics. . . .

THEOSOPHY, n. An ancient faith having all the certitude of religion and all the mystery of science. The modern Theosophist holds, with the Buddhists, that we live an incalculable number of times on this earth, in as many several bodies, because one life is not long enough for our complete spiritual development; that is, a single lifetime does not suffice for us to become as wise and good as we choose to wish to become. To be absolutely wise and good— that is perfection; and the Theosophist is so keen-sighted as to have observed that everything desirous of improvement eventually attains perfection. Less competent observers are disposed to except cats, which seem neither wiser nor better than they were last year. The greatest and fattest of recent Theosophists was the late Madame Blavatsky, who had no cat.

TRUCE, n. Friendship.

TRUST, n. In American politics, a large corporation composed in greater part of thrifty working men, widows of small means, [and] orphans in the care of guardians . . .

TSETSE FLY, n. An African insect (*Glossina morsitans*) whose bite is commonly regarded as nature's most efficacious remedy for insomnia, though some patients prefer that of the American novelist (*Mendax interminabilis*).

U

Ultimatum, n. In diplomacy, a last demand before resorting to concessions.

Universalist, n. One who foregoes the advantage of Hell for persons of another faith.

V

Valor, n. A soldierly compound of vanity, duty and the gambler's hope.

"Why have you halted?" roared the commander of a division at Chickamauga, who had ordered a charge; "move forward, sir, at once."

"General," said the commander of the delinquent brigade, "I am persuaded that any further display of valor by my troops will bring them into collision with the enemy."

Virtues, n. Certain abstentions.

Vote, n. The instrument and symbol of a freeman's power to make a fool of himself and a wreck of his country.

WOMAN, n. An animal usually living in the vicinity of Man, and having a rudimentary susceptibility to domestication. . . . The species is the most widely distributed of all beasts of prey, infesting all habitable parts of the globe . . .

WORSHIP, n. Homo Creator's testimony to the sound construction and finish of Deus Creatus. A popular form of abjection having an element of pride.

X in our alphabet being a needless letter has an added invincibility to the attacks of the spelling reformers, and like them, will doubtless last as long as the language. . . .

Y

YEAR, n. A period of three hundred and sixty-five disappointments.

YOKE, n. A word that defines the matrimonial situation with precision, point and poignancy. . . .

Z

ZEAL, n. A certain nervous disorder afflicting the young and inexperienced. A passion that goeth before a sprawl.

The American Heretic's Dictionary
(Second edition, revised & expanded)

by

Chaz Bufe

A

ACADEMIC, adj. In reference to published materials, badly written.

ACCEPTABLE RISK, n. A risk to others.

ACCURATE, adj. In accord with one's opinions.

ADJUNCT, adj. Formerly "associated with" or "attached to." Today the term is used almost exclusively as a synonym for "slave," as in "adjunct faculty."

ADVENTURE, n. A disaster in retrospect, especially one involving the pain and suffering of others.

ADVOCACY JOURNALISM, n. A derogatory term applied to the writings of journalists who openly acknowledge their biases. This despicable form of journalism is to be contrasted with the admirable practice of Unbiased Reporting, practiced by journalists who have no biases, and, indeed, no viewpoint whatsoever, on any issue on which they report.

AFFIRMATIVE ACTION, n. 1) An outstandingly effective device devised by Democrats to elect Republicans; 2) A useful means of inciting workers of different races and genders to fight over crumbs, while leaving the ill-gotten gains of the parasitocracy inviolate.

ACTRESS (also ACTOR), n. An individual who waits on tables, cooks, drives taxis, cashiers, takes tickets, ushers, does temp work, and, occasionally, appears on stage.

ADVERTISING, n. The driving force behind supply-and-demand economics: the stimulation of demand for useless products through the supply of misleading claims.

AFL-CIO, n. A labor organization which is extremely effective at delivering high salaries, good health benefits, a short work week, plentiful vacation time, and numerous other benefits—to its own executives.

AGING, ger. The barely preferable of the two alternatives. As a wise, aging soul once remarked, "When I was in my twenties and woke up hungover, I'd say, 'Damn! Did I get hammered! Shit!' I quit drinking years ago, and now when I wake up it's just, 'Damn! I feel like hammered shit!'" (with a raised pint to Margaret Wander Bonanno and her amusing novel, *Preternatural*)

AGGRESSION, n. An archaic, pejorative term formerly used in reference to preemptive defense, a prudent type of military activity which has led to the long-lasting peace and prosperity of defending nations everywhere since Napoleon preemptively defended France by marching on Moscow in 1812, to Germany's preemptive defense against the Polish threat in 1939, to the well thought out U.S. preemptive actions against Iraq and its "weapons of mass destruction" in 2003.

AGITATOR, n. (usually combined with the adjective "outside," as in "outside agitator") An undesirable person who risks life and limb because of concern for social justice, with no motive of personal gain. The truly villainous nature of the agitator is revealed by comparison with the "silent majority" member, the "good citizen," who says, does, and risks nothing in the social sphere, who is motivated solely by desire for personal gain, and to whom "Justice" means a former outfielder for the Atlanta Braves.

AGNOSTIC, n. 1) An atheist who craves social acceptance; 2) A person who feels superior to atheists by merit of his ignorance of the rules of logic and evidence.

ALCOHOLICS ANONYMOUS, n. A religious organization which helps its members overcome dependence upon alcohol by developing dependence upon tobacco, caffeine, sugar, religious concepts, and ritualized meetings.

ALCOHOLISM, n. A phenomenon characterized as physical, mental, and emotional, and treated in medical settings by nonmedical personnel with a religious program in which the patient is admitted as diseased, discharged as diseased, but permanently recovering and never recovered. (Vince Fox's excellent definition, and, in this lexicographer's opinion, the last word on the subject.)

ALIVE, adj. Seething with resentment.

AMBITION, n. The desire to tread on others.

LOVE IT OR GET OUT

AMERICANISM, n. 1) The desire to purge America of all those qualities which make it a more or less tolerable place in which to live; 2) The ability to simultaneously kiss ass, follow your boss's orders, swallow a pay cut, piss in a bottle, cower in fear of job loss, and brag about your freedom.

AMERICAN, adj. 1) Shoddy; 2) Impoverished; 3) Obsolescent; 4) Unemployed (as in "American workers").

AMERICAN PEOPLE, n. One explanation for the previous term—a rabble which, collectively, would have trouble finding its ample butt with both hands.

As H.L. Mencken so accurately, yet so poetically, put it many decades ago: "The American people, taking one with another, constitute the most timorous, sniveling, poltroonish, ignominious mob of serfs and goose-steppers ever gathered under one flag in Christendom since the end of the Middle Ages."

Putting the matter less poetically but more succinctly, Ralph Waldo Emerson noted: "In America the geography is sublime, but the men are not."

ANARCHY, n. The worst fear of every politician. A nightmare situation in which institutionalized violence, coercion, and extortion are replaced by free association, voluntary cooperation, and mutual aid. Fortunately, governments the world over maintain secret police, informers, provocateurs, torturers, prisons, execution chambers, and herds of obedient men armed with weapons of mass destruction to guard against this dreadful possibility.

ANTI-SEMITISM, n. 1) A blind, unreasoning hatred of Jewish people by those who fear, with good reason, that they are inferior to Jews. (This is not to say that Jews are inherently superior to anyone else, even anti-semites; rather, that Jewish culture encourages self-responsibility, social responsibility, learning, dedication to goals, and individual achievement—things sorely lacking in the mainstream of American culture. Hence Jews tend to be perceived as threatening "overachievers" in comparison with average, "fetch me another beer, Bubba" Americans.) 2) As defined in the United States for the last half century, the unspeakable act of criticizing the oppression of one semitic people by another (the Palestinians by the Israelis). Needless to say, this leads to gross confusion of those who seek social justice with actual anti-semites—which is precisely the intention of those who use the term in this sense. (Curiously, many of these individuals are apparently Irish, as virtually all readily respond to the name, "McCarthy.")

APARTMENT BUILDING, n. A means of extortion, the chief advantage of which is that the sheep which fall victim to it are shorn by a shears known as "rent," perhaps the most efficient means ever devised of obtaining money while performing no useful work. Further advantages are that the owner of the shears, the extortionist or "landlord," runs absolutely no legal risk and does not even need to compel the sheep to submit to their monthly shearing, that function being performed at public expense by an enforcer known as the "county sheriff."

APHRODISIAC, n. A stimulant of sexual desire. For most Americans, the aphrodisiac of choice is the rich, arousing odor of police and military boot leather. See also "Tongue."

ARSON, n. An indication of cash flow problems.

ASSHOLE, n. The most commonly employed word in American English. Frequently used by both sides in an argument, more often than not, accurately.

ARTIST, n. One to whom it is unwise to lend money.

ASS KISSING, ger. See "How to Succeed in Business Without Really Trying."

ASSAULTING AN OFFICER, ger. A legal charge resulting from a vicious attack on six uninjured, beefy cops by an unarmed, 150-pound assailant suffering bruises, abrasions, broken bones, and internal injuries. While such assaults are common, it remains a mystery as to why, invariably, the only witnesses to such attacks are the assaulted police officers. See also "Resisting Arrest," "Reasonable Force," and "Perjury."

ASTROLOGY, n. 1) A convenient means of making a living for those otherwise unemployable, safer than loan sharking or prostitution, though not as prestigious; 2) According to its practitioners, a branch of science to which it is grossly unfair to apply the normal standards of science.

ATHEIST, n. A person to be pitied in that he is unable to believe in things for which there is no evidence, and who has thus deprived himself of a convenient means of feeling superior to others.

ATOMIC WEAPONS, n. pl. Weapons of terror which have killed at least a quarter of a million people and given nightmares to whole generations of children. While some feel that the trillions of dollars spent on these weapons and their delivery systems could have been better invested in education, housing, health care, population control, job training, and feeding the hungry, it should be remembered that atomic weapons have kept the peace for half a century—except in Afghanistan, Algeria, Angola, Armenia, Azerbaijan, Bosnia, Cambodia, Chad, Chechnya, The Congo, Croatia, Cuba, Cyprus, East Timor, Egypt, El Salvador, Eritrea, Ethiopia, The Falklands, Grenada, Guatemala, Honduras, Hungary, India, Iran, Iraq, Israel, Jordan, Korea, Kosovo, Kurdistan, Kuwait, Laos, Lebanon, Libya, Mozambique, Nicaragua, Pakistan, Palestine, Panama, Rwanda, Saudi Arabia, Serbia, Somalia, Sudan, Syria, Tibet, Vietnam, Western Sahara, Yemen . . . (with apologies to a writer, whose name I've forgotten, who pointed this out in *Freedom* many years ago)

ATTRACTIVE, adj. 1) Old, fat, bald, impotent—and incredibly wealthy. This definition, of course, refers only to those qualities most women find attractive. For most men, the attractive qualities run as follows: vain, frivolous, selfish, shrewish—and having a great rack. (Our apologies for the gratuitous crudity; we meant "having a great personality.") 2) As used in personals ads by both sexes, "not hideous."

AUTOMOBILE, n. For most women, a means of transportation. For most men, an indication of penis envy (or, more charitably, a metallic penis extension). In regard to male car owners—in particular sports car, hot rod, "boom car," 4X4, SUV, pick-up, and, especially, "Hummer" owners—it's safe to say that the larger and more potent the symbol, the smaller and more impotent the symbolized.

AVENGE, v. To prolong a conflict.

AVERAGE, adj. Of poor quality, as in "the average man" and "average IQ."

B

BAD FAITH, adj. phr. A redundant modifier occasionally inserted, as if for comic effect, before the words "lawsuit" and "prosecution."

BANK, n. A pillar of the American economic system, a bank serves the needs of the working poor in the same manner that a pack of hyenas serves the needs of a wounded water buffalo.

BAR OF JUSTICE, n. A common malapropism often used as a synonym for "court of law." When used in this sense, the proper form of the term is "bar *to* justice."

BARGAIN, n. An incredible buy on something you will never, ever use. (Chalk this one up to the well known wit, Anonymous.)

BASEBALL, n. As played in the National League, the One True Faith. The dumbed-down version played in the American League merits discussion as little as it merits the designation "baseball."

BASKETBALL, n. Proof that childhood glandular disorders need not impair adult earnings potential.

BELIEF, n. 1) As commonly used, a religious term meaning "wishful thinking." This definition should come as no surprise, given that many religious folk have so little respect for facts, so little understanding of logic, and (for good reason) so little confidence in their abilities to evaluate evidence and theories that they actually maintain that one can *choose* one's beliefs. 2) As uncommonly used, a religious term meaning actual belief, that is, acceptance of a proposition as literally true and acting in accord with that acceptance. To put this another way, as the hosts of "The Man Show" did recently (in reference to Heaven's Gate and The People's Temple), "cutting off your balls and drinking the Kool-aid—*that's* belief."

BEREAVEMENT, n. A feeling of anguish caused by the death of a loved one or, more often, the reading of a will.

BERET, n. A favored means of calling attention to one's baldness. Less striking than the "comb over," but equally effective.

BESTIALITY, n. Sick, perverted sex between a human being and a registered Republican.

BIAS, n. A pejorative term normally used in reference to journalists, meaning: 1) The reporting of facts which are embarrassing to the powers that be; 2) The ability to draw obvious conclusions from observed facts, especially when those conclusions appear in print.

BIBLE, n. According to Albert Ellis, a tome which, despite having a few good parables, is "one of the crappiest self-help books ever written."

BISEXUAL, adj. Having a very good chance—in fact, twice the national average—of finding a date on Saturday night. (with apologies to Woody Allen, who we think was the originator of this chestnut, but in somewhat different form)

[TO] BLAME, v. A popular christian mass participation sport involving real or perceived social problems. This sport, termed "assigning blame," is far more enjoyable than the tedious task of actually solving social problems, especially so in that assigning blame almost inevitably leads to an even more enjoyable and morally uplifting activity—the infliction of pain. See also "Regrettable Necessity."

BOMB, n. A means of persuasion. When employed by those in power, its use is customarily termed "in the national interest,"and those who use it are customarily described as "tough" and "courageous." When employed by those out of power, its use is customarily termed "terrorism," and those who employ it are customarily described as "ruthless" and "cowardly."

BOOTLICKING, ger. A popular American mass participation sport which is rapidly displacing baseball as "the national pastime."

BORDER DISPUTE, n. (also called "Territorial Dispute" and, occasionally, "Border Skirmishing") A rumble between armed gangs controlled by national governments or other criminal organizations. Synonym: "Turf War."

BORED, adj. See "Employed."

[TO BE] BORN AGAIN, v. One of two physiologically impossible acts normally associated with fundamentalist christians. Fundamentalists claim to have already participated in one of these impossible acts, and one can't help but hope that they will soon, collectively, perform the other upon themselves.

BROWN, adj. A nose color favored by government and corporate executives.

BUDDHISM, n. A philosophy which promotes compassion, respect for life, logic, and reason, and hence in no way, but for its unfortunate embrace of self-denial, deserves to be libeled as a "religion."

BUSH, G.W., scmbg. (*Warmongerus Idiotus*) 1) Thief in Chief—from corporate criminal to war criminal in only four years (with a tip of the pinhead to Chris Carlsson and J.R. Swanson); 2) Proof that not even "differently abled" status in the fields of intelligence, compassion, honesty, and integrity can stand in the way of determination, inherited wealth, Saudi oil money, elite family connections, and a compliant corporate media. Synonym: "Commander in Thief" (with thanks to the anonymous wag who came up with that tag).

C

CANNIBALISM, n. The ultimate form of recycling.

CAPITAL, n. Dead labor, the function of which is to deprive living labor of its products.

CAPITAL PUNISHMENT, n. The killing of individuals by government agents for real, concocted, or imaginary offenses. As Senator Orrin Hatch so cogently put it, "Capital punishment is our society's recognition of the sanctity of human life."

CAPITALISM, n. Humanity's greatest achievement in the field of economics, capitalism ensures the common well-being by pitting one against all in a life-or-death struggle for economic survival. See also "Invisible Hand."

CAT, n. A small furry animal with human servants.

CAT OWNER, n. An amusing, though common, oxymoron.

CAUSE, n. (normally preceded by the article "the" and sometimes capitalized, as in "The Cause") A fine reason to sacrifice oneself, and an even finer reason to sacrifice others.

CELIBACY, n. The most unnatural perversion. (attributed to both Anatole France and Aldous Huxley)

CENSORSHIP, n. Suppression of an idea with which one agrees. Amusingly, a few obtuse types actually believe that the statement in the First Amendment, "Congress shall make no law . . . abridging the freedom of the press," actually means what it says, but this is obviously not so, as the Supreme Court has demonstrated on many occasions.

CHOSEN PEOPLE, n. See "Master Race."

CHRISTIAN, adj. Infallible in determining the morality of conduct, especially that of others.

CHRISTIAN, n. One who generously seeks to transfer his expertise in morality into provisions in the penal code.

CHRISTIAN BASHING, ger. (also called "Anti-Christian Bigotry") The despicable act of criticizing christians or christianity, and a prime example of how unbelievers victimize christians. During the Middle Ages, the unbelievers guilty of this offense included Jews, "heretics," and "witches" (especially those with, shall we say, fiery dispositions); and during modern times they include feminists, pot smokers, atheists, gay people, erotic artists, the sexually active, and other immoral malcontents denying devout christians the freedom to live in a "sin-free America" ruled by "christian principles," much as during the 1920s fascist-bashing Jews denied devout Nazis the freedom to live in . . . . . well, let's not belabor the point.

Instead of ungratefully criticizing their christian benefactors, contemporary moral degenerates should remember "no pain, no gain," and should thank their spiritual betters who are generously attempting to help them overcome their moral failings through the installation of "biblical principles" in the penal code. Sadly, this is unlikely to happen, and moral miscreants will doubtless continue to selfishly live their own lives, no matter how upsetting or "oppressive" their would-be christian benefactors may find this—and these ungrateful ne'er-do-wells will also doubtless continue to verbally "bash" the very christians who selflessly (via their police agents) employ midnight raids, imprisonment, torture, and executions in sincere, last-ditch attempts to save them from themselves.

CATHOLICISM, n. A popular form of self-degradation involving ritual cannibalism.

CHRISTIANITY, n. A form of mass narcissism. Adherents to this curious creed actually believe that the "creator of the universe" has nothing better to do with its time than to obsess over their sex lives in order to judge whether they're fit for "salvation." The more pious christians are apt to label the feeling inspired by this divine attention as "humility."

CHRISTMAS, n. A day of mourning set aside to commemorate a disaster which befell mankind, and more especially womankind, two millennia ago.

CIVIL LIBERTIES, n. pl. 1) According to conventional political wisdom, a dire threat to our nation's freedom; 2) Sacred rights which are best left unused, lest we "abuse" them and lose them.

CIVIL WAR, n. An almost unimaginable national tragedy which left the South attached to the rest of the nation.

CLASSIC, n. In regard to literature, "something everybody wants to have read, and nobody wants to read." (according to Mark Twain)

COAT HANGER, n. A popular "pro-life" religious symbol. See also "Life," "Pro-Life," and "Right to Life."

COLLATERAL DAMAGE, n. A military term referring to dead and maimed civilians. See also "Regrettable Necessity."

COMMODITY, n. In the United States, a synonym for "person."

COMMON SENSE, n. An extremely valuable commodity, as scarce in one's neighbors as it is abundant in oneself.

COMMUNISM, n. A political system based upon the revoltingly immoral belief that the ends justify the means. This concept is, of course, utterly foreign to the governing philosophy of American political parties and public servants.

COMPASSION, n. Mercy. A virtue so rare in christian countries that when discovered by chance it is always deemed newsworthy.

COMPETITIVE PRICES, n. (also "Competitive Rates") An advertising term used by long distance providers and other corporations to indicate that they charge more than their competitors.

COMPULSORY NATIONAL SERVICE, n. A civilian form of conscription promoted and much admired by liberals. Their reasoning is that enslaving American teenagers, paying them starvation wages, and forcing them to mindlessly obey orders, no matter how idiotic, will mold the nation's young people into ideal citizens of our free society.

CONDOM, n. According to the Catholic Church, a monstrously evil device, the regular use of which will deny a woman the joy of giving birth to 15 to 20 children and of devoting 26 hours a day to their care.

CONGRESS, n. 1) According to Mark Twain, the only "distinctly native American criminal class"; 2) According to IRA graffiti, the political wing of the U.S. military.

(Okay, okay—let's not quibble; the IRA said this about the British parliament and military, but the meaning is essentially the same.)

CONSCIENCE, n. A barrier to success. (Herbert Spencer's excellent definition which was written over a century ago, and which has been amply confirmed by time)

CONSENSUS DECISION MAKING, n. An ingenious tool devised by leftwing groups to advance the interests of their rightwing adversaries through the induction of self-paralysis.

CONSERVATISM, n. The desire to conserve wealth and power at any cost (to others).

CONSTRUCTIVE CRITICISM, n. The two words in American English most likely to be found in hypocritical statements, as in "I appreciate constructive criticism."

CONTINUAL GROWTH, n. The ideal state of health for multinational corporations and other carcinomas.

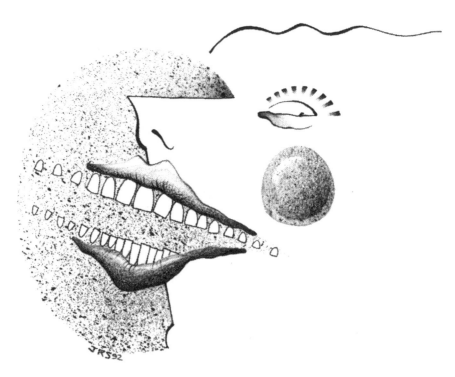

COSMETICS, n. Products designed to hide women's natural beauty while draining their pocketbooks. As demonstrated by the ex-wife of a well known televangelist/felon, the most popular types of cosmetics are properly applied with a trowel.

COURAGE, n. As commonly conceived in the United States, a military virtue. More specifically, the willingness to follow orders rather than one's conscience and to murder on command (often while running little or no risk of personal injury).

COURAGEOUS, adj. A term useful in describing one's own actions or the actions of those in positions to do one favors. In regard to physical actions, it refers to the risking of life and limb in pursuit of a goal of which one approves. This is only subtly different from the concept of "foolhardiness" (a term never applied to one's own actions), which refers to the risking of life and limb in pursuit of a goal of which one disapproves.

COWARDICE, n. A charge often levelled by all-American types against those who stand up for their beliefs by refusing to fight in wars they find unconscionable, and who willingly go to prison or into exile in order to avoid violating their own consciences. These "cowards" are to be contrasted with red-blooded, patriotic youths who literally bend over, grab their ankles, spread their cheeks, submit to the government, fight in wars they do not understand (or disapprove of), and blindly obey orders to maim and to kill simply because they are ordered to do so—all to the howling approval of the all-American mob. This type of behavior is, of course, commonly termed "heroic."

COWBOY, n. 1) As traditionally defined, a man who requires the help of a horse to outsmart a cow; 2) In modern parlance, an urban redneck who drives a pickup, affects western wear, knows as little about horses as the average lexicographer, and whose only interest in cattle is, presumably, sexual.

CRITICAL THINKING, ger. A dangerous, disturbing activity which is systematically discouraged by the U.S. education system. Fortunately, discouragement is the one thing at which the U.S. education system excels; thus, so little of the above-mentioned dangerous, disturbing activity occurs in the United States that it merits no further discussion.

CROP CIRCLES, n. pl. Proof positive that sophisticated, technologically advanced aliens routinely travel trillions of miles to indulge in a saturnalia of cattle mutilation, cornfield decoration, and anal probe implantation.

CRUELTY, n. The most important and highly valued element in entertainment in christian countries, especially in entertainment provided by the legal and penal systems. Curiously, before inflicting especially atrocious—and therefore especially enjoyable —acts of cruelty, judges and other officials in christian lands often issue statements commencing with "Regrettably we must . . ."

CULT, n. 1) An unsuccessful religion; 2) A pejorative term employed by members of religious bodies to refer to other religious bodies.

CYNIC, n. One who invariably ascribes the worst possible motives to the actions of other human beings. Synonym: "Realist."

D

DANCING, ger. According to one fundamentalist preacher, "a vertical expression of a horizontal desire."

DEATH, n. For christians, a blessing—the gateway to heaven, the portal to paradise. It speaks volumes of the generosity of christians that they so freely bestow this blessing upon their enemies, yet routinely do all in their power, even in extreme old age, to deny this same blessing to themselves.

DECONSTRUCT, v. A code word used by the insufferably pretentious in order that they might easily recognize each other. Inasmuch as the exact meaning of this term is somewhat unclear, this lexicographer would suggest that those not attempting to build literary or academic reputations use the simpler and more precise "analyze." (with a tip of the hat to Michael Albert, who, I believe, first pointed out the superiority of "analyze" decades ago in Z Magazine)

DEEP ECOLOGY, n. A polluted current in the environmental movement which draws its name from the cliche, "deep as a pie plate." "Deep" ecology ignores social, political, and economic causes of environmental problems and posits that human beings as such —never mind who they are or what they're doing—are the cause of all ecological problems. In other words, "deep" ecology lets the corporations and governments responsible for ecological carnage off the hook, while providing "deep" ecologists with a satisfying feeling of moral superiority over the rest of humanity. Thus, "deep" ecologists have publicly welcomed the AIDS epidemic and have posited that human beings are no more important, and somewhat less desirable, than tapeworms and the HIV virus. The most convincing evidence to support this belief is, unsurprisingly, provided by the "deep" ecologists themselves. Synonym: "Deep Ignorance."

DEFEND, v.t. In the United States, a new, expansive definition of this ancient term has taken root in recent years. Whereas in many benighted lands it still retains its narrow, antiquated meaning—to resist physical aggression—the up-to-date U.S. definition is much broader: to use the coercive apparatus of the state to intrude into the private lives of those one dislikes, as in the "Defense of Marriage Act." (It must be admitted, however, that this "defensive" act is rather atypical, as in this instance "cultural conservatives" are merely attempting to restrict the legal rights of those they dislike rather than jail or execute them.)

Not to give undue credit, the American religious right—not withstanding its preeminent role in modern times—is far from being solely responsible for the broadened, more versatile meaning of the term; other religious believers in other lands have used "defend" in a nearly identical manner since time immemorial. To cite but one example, a famous author sitting in a jail cell in Bavaria in 1924 used the term as follows, in what was to become a best-selling book: "By defending myself against the Jews, I am fighting for the Lord."

And, yes, you've guessed the author's identity.

DEMOCRACY, n. 1) The bludgeoning of the people, by the people, for the people. (Oscar Wilde's superb definition from *The Soul of Man Under Socialism*) 2) The reason why the U.S. government supports coups and invades third world countries, the theory being that these countries are too backward to achieve democracy on their own and require the help of the U.S. military and intelligence agencies. While historical investigation reveals that the real reasons for these coups and invasions—installation of authoritarian regimes subservient to U.S. business and political interests—have invariably been other than the stated reasons, one can rest easy knowing that these base motives no longer apply. While "mistakes have been made," current U.S. support for coups and invasions of small countries are carried out for the purest, most altruistic reasons and will indeed bring about the desired "democratic" results.

DEMOCRATIC PARTY, n. 1) The "good cop" in the biennial good cop/bad cop mugging of the American public—an abusive routine which has become such a blindly accepted, "normal" part of American life, that many working people actually believe that the "good cop" is their friend; 2) A political party which has persevered and prospered for over two centuries without, curiously, ever having had any principles to betray.

DEN OF THIEVES, n. See "Bush (or other current) Administration."

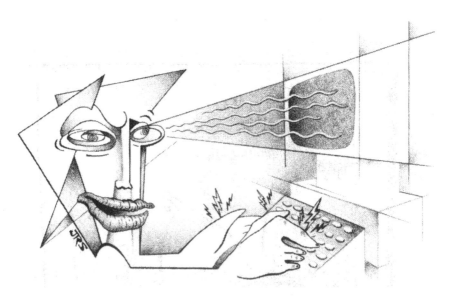

DESKTOP PUBLISHING, n. A huge advance in communications technology, desktop publishing has put within the reach of nearly everyone the ability to produce hideous-looking printed materials. Thanks to this computer-age marvel, aspiring graphic artists have attained the ability to demonstrate why they are "aspiring" almost instantaneously.

DESIGNATED HITTER, n. See "Antichrist."

Depression, n. Anger without enthusiasm. (according to Norma M., quoted in *Modern Drunkard Magazine*)

Desperate, adj. See "Single."

Despondent, adj. See "Married."

Devout, adj. 1) Placing a higher value upon dogma than upon human happiness, especially that of others; 2) Unwilling to let facts stand in the way of belief.

Dictatorship of the Proletariat, n. A theological term. It is paralleled by the Catholic belief in transubstantiation. Both are contrary to everyday experience, physically impossible, and as unthinkable as a herd of cats.

Different, adj. The same. As in, "Trust me. Things will be different this time."

Dignity, n. A term which merits little discussion, as its use is invariably inappropriate when employed to describe persons or things American, unless preceded by the words "lack of."

Dis, v. (or "Diss") As Bierce remarked upon the slang of his day, "the grunt of the human hog." One might add that while it would be easy to dismiss, disparage, disavow, disregard, discourage, or disrespect those who employ this disreputable, disconcerting usage, it serves those who grunt it quite well in that it allows them to discard the dismal, dismaying, disagreeable task of distinguishing between any number of distressingly dissimilar terms.

Distinguished, adj. An oblique term of praise, in that—at least as regards politicians, professors, and journalists—it usually means "nearly dead."

Ditto, n. A symbol indicating: 1) The same as; 2) A duplicate; 3) A thing devoid of originality. Of late, the term has acquired an additional connotation and is now commonly used as a synonym for human excrement, as in the term "dittohead," a term as ugly as that which it describes.

DRUG ADDICTION, n. A popular method of dealing with day-to-day living in the United States.

Divorce, n. Escape from the frying pan of social and sexual bondage into the fire of dire economic need.

Dog, n. A whining, biting fleabag, all too often found lurking beneath the dinner table rather than properly prepared upon it.

Doggerel, n. Poetry. Some would argue that the qualifiers "tasteless," "obvious," and "boring" should be added to this definition, but your humble lexicographer prefers to avoid redundancy.

Draft, n. Conscription. A form of slavery necessary to preserve American freedom.

Drug Kingpins, n. pl. The scum of the earth. Individuals who willingly sacrifice the lives of others in a mad rush for profit at any price. The worst of the lot are distastefully referred to as "tobacco executives" and "distillers."

Drugs, n. pl. 1) Substances which perform the same functions as religion, but with worse physical side effects; 2) Chemicals which induce madness in the police, judiciary, and legislators (with a tip of the hat to Ambrose Bierce, whose definition of "Rum" inspired this); 3) The cause of all societal problems. Not to be confused with harmless substances such as alcohol and tobacco.

Drummer, n. A guy who hangs around with musicians. (with a rim shot in honor of the anonymous wit—probably a drummer—who came up with this golden oldie)

Duty, n. A concept of slaves, a tool of tyrants. Doing what others want you to do because they want you to do it. (to paraphrase Oscar Wilde)

DRUNKENNESS, n. A temporary but popular cure for Catholicism.

E

EAGLE, n. A large, carnivorous bird which swoops upon smaller, unsuspecting animals. Once its prey is in its clutches, the eagle proceeds to tear apart its still-living victim limb from limb. When live prey is unavailable, the eagle will happily feast upon carrion. Thus, the eagle is the natural—some would say the only—choice as the official symbol of the U.S. government.

EDUCATION, n. In the United States: 1) A means of deadening the curiosity of the young; 2) A type of Pavlovian conditioning utilizing bells and buzzers, interspersed with domination and submission rituals.

EEL, n. A slimy, cold-blooded, snake-like creature which has provided inspiration to entire generations of district attorneys.

EGOMANIA, n. A disagreeable condition which afflicts others, especially the teeming masses of one's inferiors.

EGOTISTICAL, adj. Insecure. A term applicable to others.

ELDER STATESMAN, n. A politician too decrepit to do much further harm.

ELECTION, n. In the United States, the biennial opportunity to choose the apparently lesser of any number of evils.

ENEMY, n. See "Federal Government." With all due respect, Walt Kelly's famous saying from "Pogo," "We have met the enemy and he is us," is a bit off the mark. It would be more accurate to state: "We have met the enemy and he is (the) U.S. (government)."

ENTITLEMENT, n. An agreeable sensation akin to self-satisfaction experienced by pickpockets, aggressive panhandlers, ex-spouses, and IRS agents when contemplating the contents of your wallet.

EPISCOPALIANISM, n. Catholicism Lite.

ETHICAL, adj. An archaic term. In the world of commerce it has been supplanted to some extent by the concept "legal," and to a greater extent by the concept "detectable."

EUPHEMISM, n. A staple of American speech, euphemisms ooze from the lips into the air much as bilge oil from a derelict freighter oozes from a scummy discharge pipe onto the waves of the sea. The function of these slimy terms is to obscure rather than to illuminate, and motivations for their use fall into two categories: on the one hand, they are used to deceive; and on the other, they function as a primitive form of magic which attempts to change the nature of unpleasant realities by changing their referent terms. Thus, the transformation of the War Department to the Department of Defense, and the transformation of "cretin" to "exceptional child."

EVIL EMPIRES, n. pl. One down, one to go. (with thanks to the anonymous realist who came up with this at the fall of the Soviet Union.)

EXCLUSIVE TV OFFER, n. Something so incredibly bad that even the "dollar store" won't carry it.

EXISTENTIAL DESPAIR, n. Worrying in its most advanced state. (according to Bill Griffith—from the wonderfully inventive comic, *Griffith Observatory*)

EXISTING SOCIALISM, n. 1) The form of capitalism in which the state is the sole employer; 2) A term which, fortunately, is rapidly becoming archaic.

EXPERIMENTAL, adj. In relation to the arts, obscure, incomprehensible. A term applied to the works of those who invent new and startling ways to demonstrate their incompetence.
    This is not to suggest that all experimental works are artistically worthless—far from it. Only 90+ percent of such works lack merit, a percentage in keeping with the historical record. When most people contemplate even the second-rank masterpieces of the past, in the fields of music, visual art, or literature, they tend to forget that they're only seeing (or hearing) the tip of the iceberg; they don't give a thought to the huge, indeed astounding, number

of execrable—and now mercifully forgotten—works produced in past centuries.

Many years ago, a relatively enlightened optimist estimated that "90 percent of everything is shit." While we sympathize with his generous sentiments, we disagree with his overly optimistic assessment. The true percentage is about nine points higher.

EXPERTS, n. pl. Those in agreement with the speaker, as in, "Experts agree . . ."

EXTORTION, n. The extraction of money through intimidation or threat of force. Not to be confused with the "service" rendered the public by the IRS.

FACT, n. For most people, a nuisance, an obstacle to Belief—but one they find easy to overcome.

FAITH, n. An attribute of desperation. An attempt to make the intolerable tolerable. When achieved, it gives its holders a satisfying feeling of superiority over those so unfortunate as to see things as they are.

FAMILY, n. A traditional means of passing on neuroses from generation to generation.

FASCISM, n. Communism with flashier uniforms, a more efficient economic system, and an equally admirable respect for human rights.

Fascist, adj. 1) A term used by leftists to describe the corporate-state political/economic systems of Mussolini's Italy and Hitler's Germany, the key features of which were strident nationalism, militarism, a dictatorial leader with a personality cult, regimentation of industry, suppression of independent trade unions, suppression of civil liberties and all forms of political opposition, and an aggressive, expansionist foreign policy; 2) A term used by leftists to describe anything they happen to dislike—especially other leftists.

Fat Liberation, n. An attempt to make socially acceptable the visual consequences of the typical American diet and exercise regimen (more accurately, the lack of such a regimen). See also "People of Size" and "Land Whale."

FBI, n. The acronym of the U.S. government's political secret police—the American equivalent of the East German and Russian acronyms STASI and KGB. Many believe that the letters stand for Fabricate, Burglarize, Infiltrate, though it's just as likely that they stand for Frame, Blackmail, Intimidate.

Fear, n. The wellspring of religious devotion—the greater the fear, the greater the "faith." Christians normally refer to the behavior instigated by this inspiring emotion as "moral conduct."

Federal Government, n. See "Organized Crime."

Fidelity, n. Sexual exclusivity—the virtue of those so unattractive as to have no hope of sex outside of marriage.

Financially Secure, adj. 1) As used by women in personals ads in reference to men: "must be ready and willing to support me in the manner to which I wish to become accustomed"; 2) As used as a self-descriptive term by men in personals ads: A) "desperate enough to support you in the manner to which you wish to become accustomed"; and/or B) "exchanging my soul for the money seemed like a good idea at the time."

FINE, adj. A routine means of evading the question, "How are you?" This attempted evasion is not, however, entirely successful, as it's common knowledge that "fine" is an acronym that stands for Fearful, Insecure, Neurotic and Evasive. (This definition is not original; who came up with it is anybody's guess.)

FLEDGLING DEMOCRACY, n. A State Department term referring to Latin American countries whose economies are controlled by U.S.-based multinational corporations and in which voters are free to choose between a variety of rightwing parties with military ties.

FOLK MUSIC, n. In the United States, a rudimentary variety of acoustic music played on $2,000 Martin guitars by down-home, folksy types from the backwoods of Boston, Manhattan, and San Francisco.

FOOTBALL, n. 1) A popular form of human sacrifice; 2) A male religious ritual. Like most other American religious ceremonies, the rite of football is normally observed on Sundays, and is, in fact, observed on approximately 20 consecutive Sundays culminating in the holiest day of the year, Super Sunday, a day on which all normal male activities—including, even, lexicography—grind to a halt. Football is distinguished from more mundane religious observances in that its celebrants normally worship a 25-to-40-inch screened deity and imbibe a ceremonial liquid known as "Bud," the symbol of which, perhaps for reasons of taste, color, and odor, is a large horse.

FORCED, past part. A term often used in political discourse (as in, "We were forced to invade . . .") meaning: 1) Voluntarily and blatantly pursuing self-interest; 2) Seeking a cover for naked aggression or other depredations.

FOURTH OF JULY, n. Independence Day. A day set aside to celebrate the throwing off of foreign tyranny and its replacement by domestic tyranny.

FREE ENTERPRISE, n. A system in which a few are born owning billions, most are born owning nothing, and all compete to accumulate wealth and power. If those born with billions succeed, it is due to their personal merits. If those born with nothing fail, it is due to their personal defects.

FREEDOM FIGHTER, n. A State Department term referring to: 1) A mercenary attempting to install an authoritarian regime friendly to U.S. business interests; 2) A heavily armed islamic fanatic who wishes to impose his religious views upon others through the use of violence.

(This last is a now archaic and nearly forgotten—and fortunately so—definition, which dredges up unpleasant memories of the $3 billion that the Reagan/Bush Administration funneled in the 1980s to such "freedom fighters" as Osama Bin Laden and what was to become the Taliban).

FREE, adj. 1) In advertising, anything bearing a hidden cost, as in "two free dinners with purchase of . . ."; 2) A descriptive term often used by subjects of repressive governments to describe themselves and their nations, as in the oft-heard oxymoronic assertion, "this is a free country"; 3) n. A self-identifying label commonly used by these same individuals, as in "the land of the free" or, more simply, "the free." When used in this manner, an acceptable synonym is "gang of slaves."

Free Offer, n. An advertising enticement analogous to a barbed hook embedded in a wriggling night crawler.

Free World, n. A term of bitter sarcasm often employed by hack fantasists.

Freedom, n. As commonly conceived in the United States, the opportunity to impose one's will upon others via "the democratic process."

Freedom of Speech, n. 1) A sacred, inviolable right which is curtailed only when the powers that be deem it expedient. Thus, freedom of speech is an excellent barometer of the ruling elite's level of insecurity: when the powers that be feel nearly totally secure, the rabble enjoy near-total freedom of speech; when the elite feel threatened, down come the clamps; and the more threatened they feel, the harder the clamps come down. 2) The inalienable right to agree with the powers that be on any and every subject. Also, the inalienable right to disagree—as long as your words have no effect whatsoever on listeners. When it appears that your words might move others to thought or action, your freedom of speech becomes "license," "sedition," "criminal syndicalism," or, lately, "support for terrorism," and it—and you—are, of course, lawfully suppressed.

(The above definitions, needless to say, do not apply to contrarian speech from the clearly deranged, which is always accorded full constitutional protection and serves as a shining example of the respect granted even the most outlandish notions in the land of the free.)

French, adj. In regard to intellectual matters, muddy, pretentious, long-winded, unreadable, and unbearable, hence highly regarded.

Friendly, adj. A descriptive term favored by dog owners. It normally means "hasn't bitten anyone recently."

Friendship, n. A term which inspires fear, loathing, and acute disappointment in American males, as in, "I wouldn't want to do anything that might spoil our friendship."

FRIEND, n. A person with whom one can share the enjoyment of another's misfortune.

FUNDAMENTALIST, n. One in whom something is fundamentally wrong—most commonly lack of reasoning ability and vicious intolerance toward those not sharing the fundamentalist's delusions. Thus, fundamentalists are especially intolerant of those able to draw obvious conclusions from observed facts, those who refuse to seek shelter in comforting falsehoods, and those who wish to lead their own lives. Members of the fundamentalist subspecies known as "Slack-Jawed Drooling Idiots" have been known to give so much of their income to "electronic churches" that they subsist on Alpo at the end of the month. In herds, fundamentalists are about as useful to society as wandering bands of baboons brandishing machetes.

The following statements, by Reverend Pat Robertson—prominent fundamentalist, Christian Coalition honcho, former presidential candidate, and close "personal friend" of both corrupt, murderous Zairian dictator Mobutu Sese Seko and corrupt, murderous Liberian honcho/war criminal Charles Taylor—provide perhaps the most revealing illustration of the fundamentalist mentality that this lexicographer has ever encountered:

"People have immortal spirits with incredible power over elemental things. The way to deal with inanimate matter is to talk to it."

. . . and . . .

"If you wanted to get America destroyed, if you were a malevolent, evil force and you said, 'How can I turn God against America? What can I do to get God mad at the people of America to cause this great land to vomit out the people?' Well, I'd pick five things. I'd begin to have incest. I'd begin to commit adultery wherever possible, all over the country, and sexuality. I'd begin to have them offering up and killing their babies. I'd get them having homosexual relations, and then I'd have them having sex with animals."

And, yes folks, these are actual, direct quotes.

FURTHER STUDIES, n. pl. The preferred method of dealing with impending ecological catastrophes.

G

GLORY, n. An exalted state achieved through participation in military operations, often by having one's guts blown out and dying in agony amidst the stench of one's own entrails.

GOD, n. 1) A three-letter justification for murder; 2) An unsavory character found in many popular works of fiction; 3) The cosmic equivalent of "The dog ate my homework"—the explanation that means "I have no explanation."

GOD'S WILL, n. A causal factor often cited by both demented mass murderers (God, of course, "told" them to do it) and religious folk following their survival of fires, earthquakes, terrorist incidents, and car, train and airplane crashes. This is an expression of the fundamentalist belief in an omnipotent God, the belief that the universe is governed by supernatural rather than by natural causes —in other words, that "God's will" determines all events, at all times, everywhere.

If true, this demonstrates that God holds a special affection for callous, conceited cretins. For if God truly determines all things, fundamentalists claiming that their survival of an air crash is a matter of divine favor, and thanking God for it, are thanking the same God who caused the mechanical failure of the plane and the deaths of their fellow passengers.

GOLF, n. The terminal stage of a wasted life.

GONADS, n. pl. A remarkable aid to vision, our gonads allow us to see in potential sexual partners redeeming features which are completely invisible to the naked eye.

GOOD INTENTIONS, n. pl. The underlying reason for the U.S. government's invasions of small countries, support of coups d'etat against elected governments, and the training of foreign militaries and police forces in the arts of murder and torture. In the short run, the results of these things are normally referred to as "restoring democracy" or "restoring stability"; in the long run, these same results are normally referred to as "tragic mistakes" (resulting, of course, from American "good intentions").

[TO] GOVERN, v. The act and art of converting public policy into private financial gain.

GOVERNMENT, n. Organized extortion, coercion, and violence, the purpose of which is to protect us from unorganized extortion, coercion, and violence.

GREEN PARTY, n. A collection of well-intentioned individuals who are attempting to emulate the convincing successes of the British Labour Party, the German Social Democrats, the French Socialist Party, and other social democratic political parties that have held state power in utilizing the machinery of government to achieve social, economic, environmental, and political justice. Greens, of course, would object to this definition, and one can't help but be touched by their sincerity when they say, "Trust us. Things will be different this time."

GROVELING, ger. See "How to Win Friends and Influence People."

GUILT, n. The preferred leftist means of manipulating the white working class into political activism, and a means particularly favored by academics and those from upper middle class backgrounds. The theory behind this is that telling people who are under constant financial stress, have no medical insurance, are one paycheck away from being on the street, and are working 40 or more hours per week at jobs they hate that they are "privileged," and that they should "examine" their "privilege," is the ideal way to induce them to altruistically "struggle" in their copious free time for the "liberation" of the "oppressed" in order that the "oppressed" might reach the same "privileged" status that they themselves are so fortunate to enjoy.

GUN NUT, n. A pejorative liberal term that refers to a farseeing individual motivated by the horrifying realization that "when guns are outlawed, only cops will have guns."

GUTLESSNESS, n. According to the savvy political strategists who have guided the Democratic Party for decades, a certain route to victory.

HARD WORKING, adj. phr. See "Impoverished."

HATRED, n. A hallmark of spiritual development. In the United States, this admirable emotion is often, and aptly, referred to as "Christian love."

HEAVY METAL, n. A type of music played at ear-damaging volume utilizing simple, banal melodies, inane, sophomoric lyrics, and seemingly endless musical masturbation on the electric guitar. The name "heavy metal" is derived from the density of the skulls of its listeners.

HEIGHT/WEIGHT PROPORTIONAL, adj. phr. As is common in personals ads, this phrase is considerably condensed. What is actually meant is "height/weight proportional—for a bowling ball."

HEMORRHOIDS, n. pl. The sentence pronounced by Judge Nature upon the crime of ingesting the average American diet.

HERBAL, adj. As commonly used in advertising, "will not and cannot work," as in "Herbal Ecstasy" and "Herbal Viagra."

HERO, n. As normally used in the corporate media, an individual who orders mass slaughter from a safe distance. Needless to say, this definition does not apply to non-American military personnel and politicians, who, when they issue such orders, are customarily referred to as "monsters."

HEROIN ADDICTION, n. Something to devote oneself to, something to "build one's life around." More physically damaging than religion, but every bit as effective.

HELL, n. A place of everlasting torment, much like the United States during an election year.

HOCKEY, n. A popular form of violence occasionally interrupted by play.

HOMEOPATHY, n. A curious but common misspelling, unusual in that it bears essentially no relation to the correct spelling: p-l-a-c-e-b-o e-f-f-e-c-t. Synonyms: "Iridology," "Acupuncture," "Reiki," "Astrology," and "the power of prayer."

HONESTY, n. 1) The road to bankruptcy. (Herbert Spencer's superb, time-tested definition); 2) An admirable character trait, often exhibited by oneself, involving the telling of unpleasant truths. It is closely related to the annoying character trait, often exhibited by others, known as "rudeness."

HUMAN, adj. 1) Lacking in common sense; 2) Having an immense capacity for self-deception; 3) Prone to self-pity.

HUMAN BEING, n. One who makes mistakes repeetedly . . . repetedly . . . re . . .

HUMAN INTEREST, adj. phr. A descriptive term often applied to certain types of newspaper, magazine, and TV "news" stories. Given the subject matter of such pieces—children trapped in wells, "bubble boys," drug-addicted celebrities, homicidal love triangles, knife-wielding wives, "bobbitized" husbands, philandering royalty, splattered-all-over-the-pavement royalty, child-molesting pop stars, etc., etc., etc.—a more appropriate descriptive term, referring to the audience rather than the subject matter, might well be "subhuman interest."

HUMILITY, n. The virtue of those with low self-esteem.

HYPOCRISY, n. The hallmark of American culture, a character trait more common even than love of football, cruelty, or bestiality, and as pervasive as credulity and imbecility combined. It is a prominent characteristic of all strata of American society—from priests who take vows of celibacy and then make careers of molesting small children, to lawmakers who loudly proclaim their devotion to individual liberty and then pass draconian laws against drug use (while simultaneously voting for subsidies for tobacco growers), to drug-addict talk-show hosts who want to send others to jail for drug use, to hippies who regard sugar as strychnine and will

HUMAN EXCREMENT, n. The most feared substance in the universe. As Jas. H. Duke has correctly noted, most people would "rather face ten tons of plutonium than half a bucket of shit, even their own."

HYPOCRISY (cont'd) . . .
rattle on for hours about the benefits of healthy living, and who will then go home to inhale the combustion products of burning vegetable matter into their lungs. As with Traditional Values, the United States would not be what it is today without this typically American character trait.

I

IGNORANCE, n. In the United States, a common cause for pride. In itself, it is a sign of "deep faith," and in conjunction with its close cousin, gullibility, it is a sure sign of the "open mindedness" that contrasts so favorably with the "close mindedness" of those who demand proof before accepting absurdities at face value. See also "Astrology," "Homeopathy," and "Science."

ILLEGAL IMMIGRANT, n. As commonly conceived, a lazy person who comes to the United States to live off welfare and who is so desperate to find a job that he will perform odious physical labor for $2.50 an hour.

IMPACT, n. A term properly applied to the results of meteorite and artillery bombardments and, in slightly altered form, to wisdom teeth. A number of years ago, however, military briefing officers began to use the term as a transitive verb in place of "affect" or "hit," and at present "impact" is commonly employed in that sense by those who wish to hide their ignorance of the distinction between "affect" and "effect."

IMPROVING HUMAN RIGHTS SITUATION, n. A State Department term used in reference to U.S. satellites ("fledgling democracies") in Latin America. As normally employed, it refers to a decrease in the number of death squad murders from 170 to 160 per month, and a corresponding reduction in the voltage applied to the testicles of political prisoners.

INCEST, n. In many parts of the Bible Belt, the most popular form of dating.

INCOME TAX, n. A particularly painful form of economic sodomy inflicted upon the public during the IRS's annual rutting season in mid-April.

INCORRUPTIBLE, adj. Devoid of power and influence.

INEVITABLE, adj. Avoidable. As in, "It was inevitable that we were forced to declare war."

INFINITY, n. Life expectancy as perceived at age 18.

INFLUENTIAL MILITANT, n. Anarchese for "leader" (a term best avoided because of its tendency to induce hand tremors, heart palpitations, and night sweats among the faithful).

INHERITANCE, n. 1) A sacrosanct institution for millennia, and an eminently worthy cornerstone of the Free Enterprise System; 2) The handing down from generation to generation of property obtained through murder, robbery, extortion, enslavement, usury, swindles, and other forms of low cunning; 3) The exclusive enjoyment of lands and other natural resources as well as all other forms of social wealth (created by the collective labor of hundreds of generations) by those who did not create these things and who, in the case of large inheritors, don't even work. The justification for all this is the theory that the sons and daughters of those who have unfairly benefitted should also unfairly benefit. See also "Traditionalist" and "Free Enterprise."

INSOMNIA, n. 1) Sleeplessness, a condition resulting from stress; 2) A major boon to the economy. Insomnia's most obvious benefits are that it provides a mass, never-ending market for dependency-producing sleep "aids" and that it leaves its sufferers too confused to analyze the reasons for their stress-induced sleeplessness and without the energy to do anything about it even if they understood the reasons for it.

Integrity, n. A severe impediment to the achievement of public office.

Intelligence, n. The human faculty that allows us to worry about the future . . . and the present . . . and the past . . . When used in reference to political and military matters, it is customarily preceded by "lack of" or "faulty." (with a tip of the hat to Earl Lee)

Internal Police Investigation, n. An inquiry into the means by which blame for a beating or murder can be shifted from its perpetrators to its victim.

Internal Revenue Service, n. A government agency which serves the people by extorting hundreds of billions of dollars from them annually under threat of force.

Inverse Relationship, n. The normal relationship between the usefulness of work and pay for it.

Invertebrate, adj. Having excellent prospects of a career in journalism.

Invisible Hand, n. Invented by Adam Smith, the theory of the "invisible hand" posits that competition in the capitalist marketplace is guided, as if by an invisible hand, to produce the greatest public good—put more baldly, that unbridled competition unerringly promotes the common well-being.

   Given that the Earth has limited land and resources, this is more than a bit like positing that the competition over a limited supply of food between hungry rats in a locked cage will promote the common well-being of the rats. More accurately, that with 10% of the rats hoarding most of the food, the competition within the bottom 90% over the remaining morsels will promote the common well-being of the bottom 90%.

Islam, n. Incontrovertible proof that Mormonism is the second worst thing on earth.

ISRAEL, n. The northernmost province of the Republic of South Africa. (with apologizes to any readers who find this comparison with such a racist, brutal state unfair and insulting to South Africa.)

Note: This is the one entry in this dictionary which, thank "god," has become at least partially obsolete since the first appearance of these definitions in 1992.

J

JAILHOUSE INFORMANT, n. According to prosecutors, a highly reliable witness who is normally accused, or already convicted, of several felonies, and whose testimony is untainted by the anticipation of personal gain. That such witnesses normally go free or receive reduced sentences after testifying is simply well-deserved recognition of their good character and reliability. One might add that this reliability is precisely why prosecutors so commonly employ jailhouse informants in weak cases which would otherwise be dismissed.

JESUS CHRIST, int. A common exclamation indicating surprise, anger, disgust, or bewilderment.

JESUS CHRIST, n. A popular fictional character. Over the years, controversy has arisen over his middle name, and even over his middle initial. Some have held that his proper name is Jesus H. Christ, with the "H" presumably standing for "Hubert." This is incorrect. His true name is Jesus F. Christ, but the vulgar presumption that the "F" stands for "Fucking" is not only tasteless, but is simply wrong. The actual appellation of this unique mythological character is the more refined Jesus Festering Christ. (thanks to Greg "Festus" Williamson for information on J.C.'s middle initial)

JEWS, n. pl. A people uncontaminated by the New Testament, but who, unfortunately, have not escaped the attentions of those who are. As Israel Zangwill stated a century ago, "The Jews are a frightened people. Nineteen centuries of Christian love have broken down their nerves."

JOURNALISM, n. See "Jingoism." (with apologies to the relatively few fully clothed, non-"embedded" journalists)

JUSTICE, n. A term of vicious mockery, as in "equal justice under the law."

KNEELER, n. In Catholic churches, a padded attachment to pews which allows worshippers to abase themselves in comfort.

KNIGHTS OF COLUMBUS, n. pl. A group of men who are not knights, are not descendants of Columbus, and for the most part do not even live in Columbus. See also "Drunkenness" and "Catholicism."

L

LAMPREY, n. A slimy, eel-like parasite with a barbed, rasp-like tongue and a sucker-like circular mouth lined with sharp teeth. The lamprey survives by boring into the flesh of an unfortunate fish and by then sucking its victim's blood until the victim dies, a process which can take years. Unsurprisingly, the lamprey is the official symbol of the National Landlords Association (NLA). The surprise is that the NLA prevailed over the IRS in a lengthy legal battle over the right to the symbol.

LAND OF THE FREE, n. A term sometimes used, for no apparent reason, as a synonym for "United States of America."

LANDLORD, n. A pillar of society as necessary to its existence as a tick is to a hound.

LAW, n. 1) An impediment to justice; 2) A pervasive and prominent form of codified coercion which intrudes needlessly and to woeful effect into the lives of individuals; 3) The basis of a legal system which provides all the justice money can buy.

The Law forbids large numbers of immoral acts which most individuals would never consider committing (e.g., fraud, robbery, murder), while at the same time it helps maintain an economic system which provides those same individuals with constant temptation to betray their own principles—thus generating continued justification for the existence of The Law and its enforcers.

LAW STUDENT, n. Proof that evolution can reverse direction. An individual undergoing the difficult devolution from human being to primitive invertebrate. Put more succinctly, scum in training.

LAWYER, n. 1) A fungus on the body politic; 2) The apex of the capitalist food chain; 3) An individual who defends the innocent and the guilty evenhandedly—as long as they hand him even amounts of cash.

LECTURE, n. In academia, a common means of ego enhancement occasionally involving the imparting of useful information. The more skilled academics, however, normally avoid this pitfall. See also "Postmodern," "Ph.D." and "Deconstruct."

LEECH, n. See "Landlord."

LEFTIST, n. An individual holding an unshakable, childlike faith in the efficacy of electoral politics, reformist governmental solutions, and the goodness of labor "leaders" and "progressive" politicians (including bearded, dissident-murdering dictators who smoke cigars, wear combat fatigues, and speak Spanish). With the rightist, the leftist shares the belief that the ends justify the means. The difference between them lies in the fact that the leftist's means and ends are usually inconsistent, given that the leftist usually desires humane ends.

LEISURE, n. A perquisite of the rich, and one to be envied. Not to be confused with the working class perquisite of "laziness."

LESSER OF TWO EVILS, n. The perennial and inspiring reason to vote for the Democratic Party's courageous, incorruptible candidates.

LEXICOGRAPHER, n. One who consoles himself by defining that which he despairs of changing.

LEGITIMATE GOVERNMENT, n. A curiously unremarked-upon oxymoron on the level of "workers' state," "compassionate conservative," or "vegetarian piranha."

The basic premise of the "legitimate government" concept is that as long as a government (an organization using coercion, the threat of violence, and often outright violence to force those within its area of domination to bend to its will) is "democratically" elected, it is "legitimate."

To put this in perspective, let's consider an island with ten inhabitants. If six of the island's residents decided to form a government and elected three of their number to make laws binding on all residents, with the new laws enforced under threat of violence or through actual violence, and if the new governing body armed itself with deadly weapons and extorted money from (that is, taxed) everyone on the island, under current concepts that island government and its acts would be "legitimate." And if it then passed laws regulating the most intimate aspects of the daily lives of everyone on the island, including those who wanted no part of the new government, and enforced those laws at the point of a gun, those laws would, in the eyes of the world, be the "legitimate" acts of a "legitimate," democratically elected government.

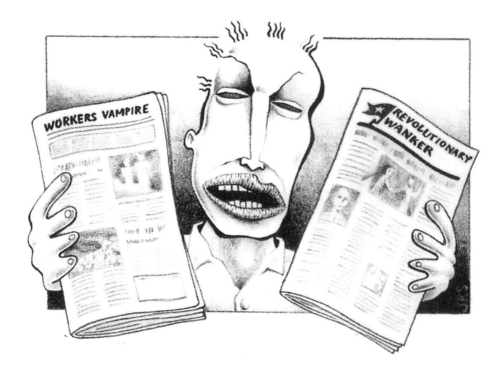

LENINIST, n. A marxist who is unable or unwilling to learn from past events. An individual who believes that a peaceful, free, and egalitarian society can be built through the systematic use of terror, violence, and coercion by a small elite. A believer in classes, but an "F" student in History.

LIAR, n. See "President of the United States." More generally, see "Public Servant."

LIBERALISM, n. The desire to liberally spend public monies.

LIBERATE, v. In conventional political terms, to free a people from the yoke of one repressive government and to replace it with another.

LIBERTARIAN, n. Formerly a synonym for "anarchist," a believer in equal liberty; the word is still sometimes used in this sense, especially in Spanish-speaking countries. Recently, however, in the United States the term has been hijacked by those who have very little in common with classical lovers of liberty (who desire equal liberty for all). It now normally refers to a member of the Libertarian Party, an altruistic person who works to ensure that all other persons have exactly (and only) the amount of liberty that their money can buy.

LIBERTARIAN PARTY, n. 1) An oxymoron; 2) A group of socially permissive Republicans (with an occasional neo-Nazi "Holocaust revisionist" thrown in for spice) who dislike paying taxes to support anything other than the repressive facets of the state (police, army, prisons, etc., a certain amount of repression being necessary to the "Libertarian" vision of "liberty"—that liberty, of course, being the liberty of the rich to pile up loot without interference from the riffraff). Not that any of this should come as a surprise, given that finding genuine libertarians in a political party is about as likely as finding hyenas dining at a vegetarian restaurant. (with thanks to Jeff Gallagher)

LIBERTY, n. In the United States: 1) The opportunity to choose a new, multi-millionaire ruler every four years; 2) The ability to exercise one's rights—an ability present in direct proportion to the size of one's bank account.

LIFE, n. 1) The highest value of "Pro-Lifers"—except when possessed by their political foes, abortion providers, or women suffering unwanted, problem pregnancies; 2) A series of minor annoyances and missed opportunities punctuated by blinding pain.

LIFE INSURANCE, n. A form of gambling in which the bettor wins if he dies before the insurer wagers that he will. This is to be contrasted with health insurance, in which the bettor never wins, full protection being extended to the bettor up to the very moment when he most needs it, and with the mandatory "insurance" sold by delivery companies, which fully protects their victims right up to the moment damaged goods arrive.

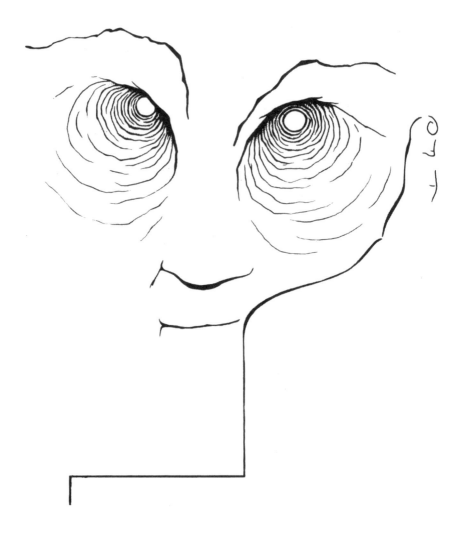

Loneliness, n. A corrosive social poison which leads those suffering its effects to seek relief via crack, alcohol, television, frantic accumulation of material goods, and, in extreme cases, habitual attendance at 12-step or other religious meetings. Synonym: "The American Way of Life."

LIMITED AVAILABILITY, n. An advertising term referring to a sale of merchandise at higher-than-average prices which will be continued until every last dollar has been wrung from the public.

LIMITED QUANTITIES, n. A nearly meaningless advertising term which means, when it means anything at all, "Please, PLEASE, *PLEASE* take one of these turkeys off our hands!"

As a moment's reflection will reveal, the term "limited quantities" is for all intents and purposes meaningless, because quantities of literally *everything* are limited, including grains of sand on the beaches of the Earth and hydrogen atoms in the universe. Thus, a person selling seawater by the teaspoon could legitimately claim "limited quantities."

LIMITED TIME OFFER, n. A sales offer limited by infinity or, more often, by the cessation of profitability.

LITERACY, n. As applied to science, music, and the English language, a concept foreign to the United States, and thus outside the scope of this dictionary.

LOAN, n. 1) In modern banking, the lending of money to those who have no need to borrow it; 2) On a personal level, an advance of money with no hope of being repaid; 3) A time-tested means of ridding oneself of unwanted "friends."

LONG TERM RELATIONSHIP, n. An indication of mutual desperation. Put less delicately, a sure sign that both partners in a conjugal relationship feel certain that they are so unattractive that, should they part, they would never, ever get laid again.

LOVE, n. 1) The recognition of another's ability to increase one's happiness; 2) The motivation of christians when they do something to someone "for their own good"; 3) A form of temporary insanity. The cure, as Nietzsche points out, often costs no more than the price of a new pair of eyeglasses.

LOWEST COMMON DENOMINATOR, adj. phr. In the entertainment industry, a term of praise meaning "admired," "sought after," "profitable." Synonyms: "Vulgar," "Box Office Smash."

LYNCH MOB, n. The purest embodiment of the principle of majority rule.

MAGGOT, n. See "Landlord."

MAJORITY RULE, n. The governing principle of the United States. The revered concept that it is every bit as right and just that 2,000,000 individuals impose their will upon 1,000,000, under threat of force, as it is that two individuals impose their will upon one, under similar threat.

As Allen Rice pointed out decades ago in *The Match!*, "Let us consider [one] of the arguments which may seem to justify taking part in [electoral] politics: 'If I take no part in government . . . then I cannot complain when it injures me.' Look at a similar situation. Suppose a group of your neighbors meet and decide to expropriate one-half of your property and income, and compel you to do manual labor for them for the next two years. Being good democrats, they are willing to put the decision to a vote and invite you to participate. Should you feel guilty if you refuse to do so? Will you have better grounds of complaint if you help vote yourself into slavery or if you do not?"

MAFIA, n. An uncommonly straight shooting group of businessmen.

MAKEWORK, n. A federally funded giveaway involving the construction of roads, bridges, parks, playgrounds, and public buildings by those who would otherwise be unemployed. This type of parasitism is to be contrasted with the useful activities of attorneys, realtors, landlords, stockbrokers, insurance salesmen, commodities speculators, tobacco executives, televangelists, tennis pros, golf pros, military officers, and narcotics agents; and under no circumstances should it be confused with the productive labor of "defense" workers—even though what there is to defend against has been a mystery for some years now, other than terrorists wielding box cutters, a threat which, needless to say, is correctly met through expenditures of hundreds of billions of dollars annually on nuclear weapons, "Star Wars" anti-ballistic-missile systems, and maintenance of hundreds of U.S. military bases in such terrorist threats as Germany, England, Italy, Japan, Panama, Guam, Iceland, The Netherlands, Thailand, Belgium, Singapore, Australia, Aruba, Denmark, Norway, Samoa, Austria, New Zealand, Greece, Spain, The Azores, The Bahamas, and Greenland.

In other words, the proper response to the box cutter threat has been to jack up American military spending to the point where it equals that of all other nations on Earth combined. While some may question these breathtaking expenditures, they are amply justified by their fruits: the remarkable tranquility and freedom from fear that characterize American society today.

MALICIOUS, adj. Admirably suited to leading a crusade for moral betterment. See also "Devout."

MARINE CORPS, n. A common misspelling. An additional "e" is necessary. The term refers to a military body which "builds men" by stripping teenage boys of all signs of individuality and by then physically and emotionally abusing them until they will unquestioningly obey orders to kill, and will enjoy doing so. The salutary effects of this training upon former marines after they return to civilian life are too well known to enumerate.

Those few readers unfamiliar with these beneficent effects can perhaps surmise them from one of the chants formerly (and perhaps currently) used in basic training at Camp Pendleton:

> One two three four
> Every night we pray for war
> Five six seven eight
> Rape. Kill. Mutilate.

MARRIAGE n. 1) A touchingly romantic ceremony in which two individuals receive permission from the state to have sex and to add to the world's population woes; 2) A means of discouraging sex. As John Rush so perceptively put it, "Marriage turns lovers into relatives."

MASS EXTINCTION, n. The periodic annihilation of up to 90% of life on Earth following the impacts of asteroids, comets, capitalism, "communism," and other (un)natural disasters.

MASS TRANSIT, n. An ecologically sound, criminally underutilized means of transport ideally suited to the transportation needs of one's neighbors.

MASTER RACE, n. A racist concept which posits that one race is superior to all others, and which thus provides a rationale for acts of mass murder and mayhem. Racist ideologues cling tightly to the "master race" theory even though convincing contradictory evidence stares them in the face every time they shave or apply make-up.

MASTURBATION, n. An extremely disgusting act performed, on a regular basis, by everyone *else*.

MAUDLIN, adj. An unnecessary term occasionally placed, by those unfamiliar with the art form, before the words "country song."

MEANNESS, n. The most common form of piety.

MENDACIOUS, adj. Having excellent earnings potential and good prospects of election to public office.

MENSA, n. 1) An organization in which the leading cause of death is the acutely swollen ego; 2) Proof that IQ alone is a poor measure of intelligence and has nothing to do with taste. The more perceptive Mensans thus tend to regard membership in the organization as a distinction commensurate with that afforded by a youthful conviction for indecent exposure.

METICULOUSNESS, n. An admirable quality in oneself. Not to be confused with "anal compulsiveness," a condition which afflicts others.

MELTING POT, n. Metaphorically, a reducing tank in a rendering plant. The end product is commonly termed "Americanism."

MONOGAMOUS, adj. Preferring to have affairs in secret.

MONOGAMY, n. A common misspelling. See "Monotony."

MIRACLE, n. 1) According to Elbert Hubbard, an event described by those to whom it was told by men who did not see it; 2) God's admission that He didn't get it right the first time.

MISERY, n. 1) An unpleasant feeling caused at times by losing a job or a relationship, though caused more often by *not* losing a job or a relationship; 2) A badge of honor among leftist political radicals (often referred to as "self-sacrifice," "altruism," or "devotion to The Cause"), the theory being that the more miserable one makes oneself, the more effective one is in eliminating misery in the rest of the world. (with thanks to someone whose name escapes me [Jon Russell?] who pointed this out years ago)

MISSTATEMENT, n. An "untruth" uttered by the president or vice-president. Not to be confused with the common "lie" told by mere mortals.

MODERATE, n. A politician for sale to the highest bidder, and much admired by journalists because of mutual resemblance. As for the moderate's principles, as Anatole France observed in *Penguin Island*, "moderates are always moderately opposed to violence." He could have added that they are also always moderately honest, moderately dignified, and moderately priced.

MODESTY, n. 1) As Schopenhauer noted, in persons of great ability, dishonesty; 2) In the sexual sense, morbid self-loathing.

MONEY, n. For many individuals, the aphrodisiac of choice. Your discreet lexicographer refrains from mentioning the gender of most such persons because of his innate sense of gallantry—*not* out of craven fear of "bobbitization."

MORAL, adj. In the conventional judeo-christian sense, anything tending to increase human misery, as in "moral conduct" and "moral standards."

MORALITY, n. As practiced in the United States, a concept related to the behavior of others.

MORMON, n. A common misspelling. Only the first "m" is necessary.

MOUNT RUSHMORE, n. An esthetic disaster in South Dakota. A desecrated mountain bearing the likenesses of four dead politicians chiseled into its flanks—in other words, graffiti "tagging" taken to its logical extreme. Every year, this unnatural wonder is reverently viewed by hundreds of thousands of camera-toting, polyester-clad Americans, a people who cherish kitsch ugliness as they do the infliction of pain.

MOTORCYCLE, n. An indication of arrested emotional development sometimes misidentified as a means of transport.

MULTIFACETED, adj. Scattered.

MURDER, n. 1) One of the most heinous crimes, and one for which there is never an adequate excuse. Not to be confused with the noble and necessary practice of killing upon government command. 2) An extreme and unnecessarily messy form of population control, though the only type that many religious folk will willingly practice.

MUSIC, n. An area of universal expertise. The less formal musical training persons have, the more certain they are to know what is "good," and the more certain they are that their opinions are just as valid as the opinions of those who have spent their lives studying, playing, and composing music.

MUSTURBATION, n. A form of self-abuse practiced by those in the habit of shoulding all over themselves. (with thanks to Albert Ellis)

MUNICIPAL ELECTION, n. In politics, a refreshing dip in an open sewer.

MYSTIC, n. A man or woman who wishes to understand the mysteries of the universe but is too lazy to study physics.

MYTHOLOGICAL, adj. A derogatory term applicable to the religious concepts of others.

N

NASHVILLE SOUND, n. 1) Arguably the dominant strand in country music, the Nashville Sound combines the musical challenge and innovation of Mantovanni with the lyricism and profundity of a greeting card; 2) Strong evidence that the average musical IQ is below 80 and falling fast. Synonym: "Hank Williams on Prozac."

NATIONAL DEFENSE, n. In U.S. political discourse: 1) The pauperization of the nation through expenditures for deadly weapons systems; 2) The bombardment and invasion of small countries. The United States is, of course, the only nation entitled to such "defense." If the inhabitants of other countries resist the U.S. government's "defensive" measures, they become guilty of "internal aggression"; and if the governments of other countries practice U.S.-style national defense, they become guilty of "naked aggression."

(An aside for younger readers: U.S. government spokesmen repeatedly used the term "internal aggression" during the 1960s when referring to the resistance of the Vietnamese to the U.S. occupation of their country.)

NATIONAL INTEREST, n. That which increases the wealth and power of the top 10 percent at the expense of the bottom 90 percent.

NATIONAL SECURITY, n. 1) An excellent reason to undertake military adventures which boost an incumbent president's reelection chances; 2) An equally excellent reason to restrict civil liberties and access to information, the theory being that the nation is "secure" and its freedom assured only when the people are unable to affect the actions of the government and do not have the information necessary to hold informed opinions; 3) A handy shield against felony indictments. (to paraphrase Gore Vidal)

NAZI GERMANY, n. A state existing in Northern Europe between 1933 and 1945 in which the government was elected to office on the basis of patriotic and nationalist appeals; the head of state was a pathological liar who attempted to present a folksy image; the government operated for the benefit of big business; civil liberties were systematically suppressed in the name of national security; the mass media was subservient to the government and to big business, and essentially operated as the government's propaganda arm; a huge military machine was constructed and was glorified as the embodiment of the highest values of the nation; small, helpless countries were the objects of invasion; a majority of the people enthusiastically supported those military adventures; there were huge disparities in the distribution of wealth and income; the rights of working people to organize were severely restricted; the unions propped up capitalism and the state; the government routinely intruded into individuals' private lives; abortion was outlawed; the government embarked on a massive prison-building spree, while locking up millions of its own citizens; and logic, skepticism, and rationality were ridiculed, while mysticism, spirituality, and "patriotism" (blind support of the government) were considered the highest virtues. In other words, a country bearing no discernible resemblance to the United States.

NECROPHILIA, n. A dark, disturbing desire for an investment banker.

NEIGHBOR, n. In apartment living, a person protected by law from bodily assault. See also "Scumbag," "Rap," and "Heavy Metal."

NEW AGE, adj. (pronounced as one word—rhymes with "sewage") 1) Having to do with money; 2) Pretentious, self-satisfied, condescending; 3) Lacking concern for the less fortunate. (with thanks to Penn & Teller for publicly supplying the correct pronunciation of this term)

New Age Music, n. Sonic Valium for those who find Muzak too "edgy."

New Ageism, n. An approach to life which posits that individuals create their own reality and are therefore "totally responsible" for everything that happens to them. Thus, individuals suffering from cancer choose to have cancer, dirt poor peasants choose to be dirt poor, the DuPont and Rockefeller heirs choose to be filthy rich, and in the 1940s six million Jews chose to be exterminated by the Nazis.

One great advantage of this solipsistic doctrine is that it allows the idle rich to feel morally superior to the working poor. Thus, new age "spirituality" is perfectly suited to the needs of its devotees—"highly evolved" members of the upper income brackets of a country in which 5% of the world's population squanders 30% of the world's resources.

The only exceptions to the "total responsibility" rule are, of course, individuals indulging in behaviors such as drinking too much, eating too much, and gambling excessively. Individuals engaging in such behaviors (commonly called "oholics" or "aholics") are, according to many new age gurus, victims of a "disease" and are thus "powerless" to change their behaviors. These same "diseased" individuals would, of course, be "totally responsible" for their own deaths were they to be hit by a truck running a red light.

New Ager, n. An adherent to new age "philosophy." As a living testament to the power of positive thinking, the new ager is every bit as powerful an example as his animal cousin, the ostrich. The difference between the two lies in the fact that while the ostrich sticks his head in the sand at the first hint of danger, the new ager sticks his head in the (metaphysical) sand at the first hint of reality.

New Year's Day, n. An arbitrarily chosen day, celebrated for its arbitrariness, in which the horrors of the previous year are forgotten in anticipation of those of the year to come.

Not Sold in Stores, adj. phr. As commonly used in television commercials, "one close look at this thing and you'd never buy it."

OBEDIENCE, n. The distinguishing characteristic of dogs, "ditto-heads," and other curs.

OBESE, adj. In the United States, a synonym for "normal looking," as in the common but redundant term, "obese Americans."

OBJECTIFICATION, n. The disgusting, degrading, and dehumanizing male practice of sizing up women sexually. As is obvious, the term should not be applied to the normal and natural female practice of sizing up men economically.

OBJECTIVITY, n. A journalistic term signifying gross servility to the powerful.

OBSCURITY, n. In regard to the arts and literature, the first refuge of the incompetent. See also "Experimental."

OFFICIAL STATEMENTS, n. pl. Self-serving lies of varying degrees of hypocrisy. (with apologies to Johnny Yen who, if memory serves, first pointed this out decades ago in *Freedom Fortnightly*)

ORGANIZATION, n. A convenient stage on which to reenact old family dramas.

OLD GLORY, n. A common misspelling. Only the first "L" is necessary. (with thanks to "Dire Wolf," aka "Spike")

P

PAIN, n. The road to christian, jewish, and muslim virtue. Admirable and eminently pleasing to god when inflicted upon oneself, exquisite and infinitely pleasing to the deity when inflicted upon others.

PARASITOLOGY, n. See "Lifestyles of the Rich and Famous."

PATRIOT, n. 1) A dangerous tool of the powers that be; 2) A herd member who compensates for lack of self-respect by identifying with an abstraction; 3) An enemy of individual freedom; 4) A fancier of the rich, arousing odor of police and military boot leather.

PARENT, n. One who is unfit to raise children. As a general rule, the more unfit the parent, the larger the number of children. See also "Catholic," "Mormon," and "Environmental Criminal."

PARENTHOOD, n. The chance to live vicariously through one's children. Unfortunately, children often spoil this unique opportunity through inconsiderate attempts to live their own lives.

PATRIOTISM, n. 1) The inability to distinguish between the government and one's country; 2) A highly praiseworthy virtue characterized by the desire to dominate and kill; 3) A feeling of exultation experienced when contemplating heaps of charred "enemy" corpses; 4) The first, last, and perennial refuge of scoundrels.

PEACE, n. The ideal state of society. As usually conceived, a condition in which the top 1 percent of the population own over 40 percent of the wealth; the bottom 50 percent of the population own essentially nothing; the environment is systematically despoiled in the pursuit of private profit; a very high percentage of the populace work long, exhausting hours at mindnumbingly dull jobs for low pay; working people fight over crumbs while divided along lines of race and gender; tens of thousands are killed and hundreds of thousands are seriously injured on the job annually; uncounted numbers succumb to job-related, chemically induced cancers; millions go uneducated, unemployed, homeless, and hungry; tens of millions lack medical insurance; good medical care is only for those who can afford it; huge masses of heavily armed men are maintained in idleness at public expense; the police and judiciary routinely and viciously intrude into the lives of individuals; and small groups of wealthy men ("public servants") impose their will ("laws") on society and have their orders enforced by violent gangs recruited from the dispossessed masses—not that much enforcement is needed given the robot-like passivity of the legendary "people." The dedicated individuals who help to maintain this salutary state of affairs are, of course, referred to as "peace officers," "clergymen," and "journalists."

PENIS, n. A male organ commonly employed in place of the brain. As the blues group Little Charlie and the Nightcats so poetically put it, the demands of this organ often lead to the "two-legged dog routine," which is a direct result of "thinking with the wrong head."

PENSION, n. The carrot dangling at the end of the stick of a wasted work life. Of late, it has become fashionable to snatch the carrot away at the last moment via "corporate restructuring," "downsizing," "outsourcing," "offshoring," and other forms of larceny.

PEOPLE OF COLOR, n. 1) A politically correct term used to refer to noncaucasian peoples—not to be confused with the politically incorrect term, "colored people"; 2) Code words through which the politically correct recognize each other.

The popularity of this term could well foreshadow an important linguistic trend—the withering away of the use of adjectives ending in "ed." If this occurs, we can look forward to constructions such as, "The little girl in the dress of stripes bought three balloons of color."

PERJURY, n. A common leisure time activity of policemen.

PERSONAL FRIEND, n. As opposed to the "impersonal friend," someone the speaker has met at least once.

PERVERTED, adj. 1) Having sexual preferences contrary to one's own; 2) Having sexual preferences similar to one's own, but lacking the discretion to conceal them.

PH.D., n. Phony Distinction. A title which the insufferably vain attach to their names in order that we might easily recognize them. The most insecure of these individuals are not content with the "Ph.D." suffix, and instead feel the need to place the title "doctor" before their names, even though they would have difficulty telling the difference between a broken arm and a case of gonorrhea.

PHILANTHROPIC, adj. Motivated by guilt.

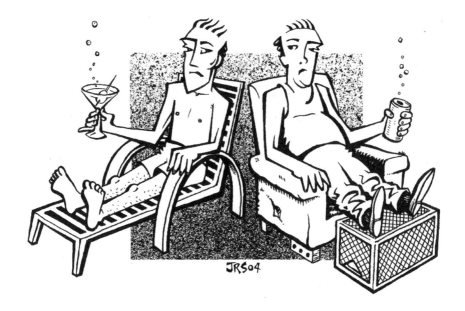

PLAYBOY, n. A high status, upper class individual who is admired and envied largely because he performs no useful work and lives off the labor of others. Strangely, the admiration and envy extended toward the playboy are not extended toward his working class counterpart, commonly termed the "bum" or "vagrant."

PHILANTHROPIST, n. One who returns part of the loot. (with thanks to Vince Williams)

PHYSICALLY FIT, adj. phr. As a self-descriptive term in personals ads, "no more than 30 pounds overweight."

PIETY, n. An uncommonly strong fear of death.

POET, n. A person who cannot write prose.

POETRY, n. An expression of narcissism. The French Poodle of the arts. Much indulged in because it is by far the easiest of the arts to do badly. See also "Experimental" and "Obscurity."

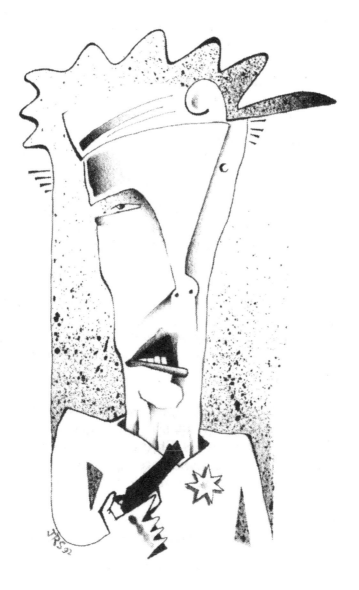

POLICEMAN, n. 1) A 22-year-old high school graduate entrusted with safeguarding the lives and well-being of the public because he can't find a better job. In terms of performance, the public gets exactly what it pays for. 2) An individual who holds others to the highest standards of the law.

See also "Perjury," "Resisting Arrest," "Assaulting an Officer," and "To Protect and Serve."

Political Dissident, n. A courageous, praiseworthy individual who challenges political and social evils in other countries. Political dissidents do not, of course, exist in the United States; instead, we are cursed with "peaceniks," "eco-freaks," "pinkos," "commies," "eco-terrorists," "outside agitators," "tree huggers," "feminazis," "unpatriotic malcontents," and "Un-American cry-babies."

Politically Correct, adj. (also termed "PC") 1) A derogatory propaganda term used by Republicans to denounce anything which could conceivably lead to a juster, freer society. This usage replaces the now archaic terms "communist," "commie," and "pinko." 2) An unfortunately all-too-real leftist phenomenon with the connotations joyless, self-righteous, deadly dull, puritanical, motivated by guilt, painfully forced, patronizing (or matronizing), more interested in form than in content, more interested in posturing than in effecting change, and (in regard to language) affected, awkward, wordy, euphemistic, and vague.

A sure test of whether or not a word or phrase is politically correct is this: If the suspect term is longer, clumsier, and less precise than the term it's intended to displace, chances are 99 out of 100 that it's politically correct; and if, in addition, it stimulates the gag reflex, chances are 99.999 out of 100 that it's PC.

Thanks to politically correct phrase-makers, the English language has already been enriched with terms such as "people of color," "differently abled," "caveperson," and "personhole cover." And if present trends continue, it won't be long until the oppressive if redundant term, "corrupt congressman," is replaced by the more respectful "morally challenged congressperson." (with apologies to the anonymous wit who came up with the "congressman" definition ages ago)

Pope, n. The world's most popular and highly paid drag performer.

Popular Taste, n. A grotesque oxymoron, as in "popular taste in music."

POSSESSIVENESS, n. A frequent adjunct of romantic interest, in which one person treats another with all the love, respect, and consideration he or she would give to a butterfly being pinned to a mounting board.

POSTMODERN, adj. Inasmuch as none of its habitual users can provide a coherent definition of this term, this lexicographer shall not attempt to do so, either. Suffice it to say that the term—although used as if to describe externalities—is, in fact, self-referential, a handy self-labeling device which spares its users the trouble of describing themselves as pretentious academic twits more concerned with impressing than with informing. Thus the function of the word "postmodern" is virtually identical to that of the names Foucault, Derrida, Deleuze, Lacan, and Lyotard. See also "Deconstruct," "French," "Ph.D." and "Lecture."

POTENTIAL, n. As commonly used in advertising (as in "unlimited profit potential" and "unlimited income potential"), anything that will remain, forever, "potential."

PRAGMATIC, adj. As used to describe politicians: 1) Hypocritical; 2) Opportunistic; 3) Inconsistent; 4) Motivated solely by self-interest; 5) Not to be trusted under any circumstances.

PRAY, v.i., The American spelling of the British "prey," as in "Let us pray." (with thanks to Earl Lee)

PRESIDENT OF THE UNITED STATES, n. 1) A pathological liar suffering delusions of grandeur; 2) An office which confers upon its holder vast coercive power as well as the means to commit mass murder—an opportunity of which all recent U.S. presidents have taken advantage. Because of this, some observers have concluded that only the worst type of individuals seek the office of president. This unkind assessment is, however, incorrect. It is much more realistic to conclude that only the worst type of individuals are *elected* to the office.

(This definition was, obviously, written in the Halcyon days of the 1990s, at which time this lexicographer naively assumed that future presidents would in fact be elected. Suffice it to say that the very worst types of individuals are not elected, but rather *selected*, to the office.)

Prayer, n. 1) A form of begging, unusual in that it's often practiced as a solitary activity. When practiced in groups, it is normally referred to as "worship." 2) A humble supplication, the premise of which is that the omnipotent, omniscient creator of the universe will benefit from the guidance of the humble supplicator.

PRESS SECRETARY, n. A White House official who lies when the president is unable to do it for himself.

PRICELESS, adj. Demanding a high price. The more priceless the object, the higher the price, as in "literally priceless."

PRIDE, n. The distinguishing characteristic of those who have honed to perfection the virtue of humility.

PRIEST, n. A holy individual who follows—often to excess—the divine injunction to "love the little children."

PRIMITIVISM, n. A millenarian ideology similar in some ways to situationism, but more religious in nature. Where situationism laments that the world today is so "dominated" by "Capital" that the socio-political situation is essentially hopeless, primitivism laments that the world today is so "dominated" by "technology" that human society is doomed unless "technology" is abandoned and humanity returns to a hunter-gatherer existence. (To fully appreciate the religious nature of this belief, substitute the word "sin" for "technology," and the words "state of grace" for "hunter-gatherer existence" in the previous sentence.) Thus the distinguishing feature of situationism is political apathy, while the distinguishing feature of primitivism is religious zeal.

Like its near cousin, "deep" ecology, primitivism is a very useful ideology in that it lets the corporations and governments responsible for environmental mayhem off the hook while providing its advocates with a satisfying and risk-free feeling of moral superiority over the rest of humanity. (Primitivism is risk free in that its premises are so ridiculous that no one expects its proponents to put their theories into practice, even on the smallest, most personal scale. So, of course, they don't; and, like other atavistic evangelists, the leading advocates of primitivism choose to live in well-heated houses in major urban areas and to make use of modern communications technologies to spread their millenarian message [which urges, among other things, the abandonment of modern communications technologies].) See also "Deep Ecology" and "Situationism."

PROCRASTINATION, n. 1) The postponement of happiness; 2) An exceptionally reliable means of ensuring at least a minimal amount of misery in one's life.

PROCTOLOGIST, n. A practitioner of political science, that is, one who studies . . . politicians. The proctologist is to be distinguished from the lobbyist and the journalist in that while all three devote their attentions to the same political objects, the proctologist, in his investigations, does not normally utilize his nose as the probing instrument.

PROFESSIONAL, n. In the fields of sex and law, an individual who takes a client's money and then screws the client. (a definition dating, for obvious reasons, from antiquity)

PROGRESS, n. An uplifting term used by Chamber of Commerce types to refer to deleterious change. The more deleterious the change, the greater the "progress."

PRO-LIFE, adj. 1) Pro-death (of political opponents, abortion providers, and women, through back-alley abortions); 2) Vitally concerned with the well-being of "babies" right up to the moment of their birth—at which time they become "welfare cases" and "future criminals" undeserving of such luxuries as housing, health care, adequate nutrition, and a decent education. This has led some unsympathetic observers to conclude that the interest of "pro-lifers" in the welfare of "babies" is purely hypocritical, and that they are, in fact, motivated primarily by misogyny and anti-sexual "moral" hysteria—that their true interest is in causing as much misery as possible to sexually active women by forcing them to carry unwanted pregnancies to term. This, however, is not the case. If "pro-lifers" truly lacked concern about the welfare of the unwanted babies born as a result of "pro-life" policies, they wouldn't be so willing—in fact, so eager—to have taxpayers shoulder the crushing costs of building the prisons necessary to house those "babies" later in their lives.

PROPAGANDA, n. A despicable misuse of language practiced in other countries. Normal propaganda terms are often euphemisms designed to disguise the nature of that which they represent, while ideal propaganda terms are both catchy and vacuous, and inspire human pawns to identify with and to do the bidding of their manipulators. Thus, observation of their fellow Americans has led some cynical observers to conclude that everyday language, as well as that used in the U.S. corporate media, is rife with propaganda terms, and that many of them originate in the White House, Congress, the Pentagon, and other arms of the federal apparatus, as well as in corporate hierarchies and ad agencies. As evidence, these cynics point to widely used titles, terms, catch phrases, and slogans, such as Internal Revenue "Service," "National Interest,"

"Free Enterprise," "Vital American Interests," "Improving Human Rights Situation," "Fledgling Democracy," "National Security," "Restoring Democracy," "Pro-Life," "Surgical Bombing," "Collateral Damage," "Americanism," "Un-American," "America, Love it or Leave it," and "Support Our Troops." This lexicographer, however, does not agree that these are propaganda terms, and instead prefers to view them as examples of the richness and vitality of the American language.

PROPHECY, n. The most gratuitous of all forms of error. (according to H.T. Poggio)

PROSECUTOR, n. A common misspelling. See "Persecutor."

PROSTITUTION, n. The sad, degrading act of renting one's body to the highest bidder. Not to be confused with the ennobling practice known as "wage labor."

PROTECTION RACKET, n. A primitive form of government. Protection rackets differ from legitimate governments in that the criminals running protection rackets are content with stealing your money and do not attempt to control your private life.

PSYCHIC, n. An individual having an uncanny, seemingly supernatural talent for extracting money from morons.

PUBLIC SERVANT, n. A government functionary who rules those he "serves."

Q

QUEEN, n. A term used in both the U.S. and the U.K. to refer to an individual. The difference lies in the fact that the British queen does not dress as well as her American counterparts.

QUIET, adj. A term of approval used by neighbors and co-workers to describe mass murderers and serial killers.

R

RACISM, n. A sign of idiocy indicating that an individual believes that other racial groups can be even worse than his own.

RACIST, adj. 1) A term applied to those sufficiently stupid and malicious (or should we say "sufficiently mentally and morally challenged"?) as to be guilty of racism; 2) In intraleftist disputes, a handy though meaningless epithet which has largely supplanted such archaic usages as "running dog" and "fascist." It is an especially useful epithet in that it almost always succeeds in diverting attention away from bothersome critical analyses and unpleasant realities (such as embezzlement of public funds), and helps to ensure adherence to politically correct orthodoxy in thought, speech, and action.

RAP, n. 1) The type of music one plays or sings when one cannot play or sing music; 2) A type of "music" usually played at ear-damaging volume, utilizing simple, repetitive rhythms, the simplest harmonic structure imaginable (more often, no harmonic structure whatsoever), and a repetitious, singsong, spoken "melody." In other words, like Heavy Metal and Country, a type of music ideally suited to the tastes and understanding of those who received (or more often didn't receive) their musical educations in the United States.

RAPTURE, n. An eagerly awaited religious event in which the world will be rid of much unwanted rubbish.

REALISM, n. Among anarchists, socialists, greens, and other political progressives, the principled reason to engage in unprincipled actions. Synonym: "Realpolitik."

REASONABLE FORCE, n. A police term which normally refers to a beating or murder witnessed only by the police. The exact meaning, however, will vary considerably depending upon the victim's race, economic status, and political connections (or lack thereof).

RECTOCRACY, n. The form of government that has replaced what once passed for democracy in the United States. The term, of course, means "government by assholes." Synonym: "Bush Administration"—and, since you asked, yes, both of them. (with thanks to "Psycho Dave" Irish)

REFORMER, n. A successful heretic. In contrast, the unsuccessful heretic is normally referred to as "the mutilated body in that unmarked grave." (thanks to Yves "Kilroy" Barbero)

REGRETTABLE NECESSITY, n. An avoidable atrocity. The term is often employed by presidents and prime ministers when announcing bombings of civilian targets and invasions of small countries.

RELATIVE, n. An individual one would never, ever choose as a friend.

RELIABLE SOURCE, n. A journalistic term referring to a politician, lobbyist, or bureaucrat with an interest in seeing certain "facts" in print.

RELIGION, n. 1) The first refuge of the desperate; 2) A convenient way of avoiding such unpleasantries as reality and independent thought; 3) A means of feeling superior to others; 4) A cult which has achieved sufficient longevity, membership, and economic clout to merit societal acceptance.

REPLACEMENT WORKER, n. A journalistic term used to protect the delicate eyes and ears of the public from the horrifying word, "scab." The term refers to an individual who has honed to perfection the virtues of greed, treachery, and servility, and who, in his employment-stealing activities, is, of course, "protected and served" by the police (at public expense).

REPUBLICAN, adj. 1) Excessively fond of Frank Sinatra, large GM automobiles, small perfumed dogs, and income produced by others; 2) Having an affinity for gold (in bullion, jewelry, and shower form); 3) Genitally underendowed. (with a tip of the rhinestone-studded Stetson to the fine magazine, *Smurfs in Hell*, which reports that a typical Republican nickname is "Needledick")

RESPECT FOR AUTHORITY, n. Lack of respect for oneself. A virtue exemplified by the adoring gaze of a dewy-eyed dog toward its beloved, though abusive, master. See also "Bootlicking."

RETIREMENT, n. Prima facie evidence that the Free Enterprise System terrorizes people so thoroughly that they "willingly" spend their lives working at jobs they hate.

RESISTING ARREST, ger. The legal charge levelled against ctizens subjected to "reasonable force" by policemen when the only witnesses to the act are other policemen. Synonym: "Assaulting an Officer." See also "Perjury."

REVENGE, n. Better than sex. The fifth member of the four food groups. The statement that "man cannot live by bread alone" is indisputably correct, though incomplete; a fuller and more accurate phrasing would be, "Man cannot live by bread alone. But throw in revenge and he'll give it a shot." See also "Avenge."

REVOLUTION, n. An oft-heard, 19th-century, millenarian term. Though it has largely lost its ability to inspire self-sacrifice, the term is still tremendously useful: when preceded by the words "after the," it is *the* perfect reason to refuse to tackle problems —especially those related to personal behavior—in the here and now.

RHYTHM METHOD, n. See "The Miracle of Birth."

RIGHT TO LIFE, n. According to "pro-lifers," the most fundamental of all human rights, though, curiously, one fully possessed only by zygotes, embryos, and fetuses induced by rape or incest.

RICH, adj. Performing no useful work.

RICHES, n. The savings of many in the hands of one. (according to Eugene V. Debs)

RIGHTWING, adj. 1) In the service of the wealthy and powerful; 2) If working for a living, having the intelligence of a dildo; 3) Having all of the warmth, compassion, and decency of a rabid hyena.

ROGUE STATE, n. A disreputable nation that: 1) develops weapons of mass destruction; 2) uses them against civilian targets; 3) arrogantly interferes in the internal affairs of other nations; 4) invades other nations under false pretexts; 5) aids and abets other aggressors; 6) trains and finances terrorists, death squads, and torturers; 7) is either an outright dictatorship or has an electoral process that makes a mockery of democracy; and 8) has a press subservient to the powers that be, so that the brainwashed masses are largely unaware of the preceding outrages. In other words, a dangerously destructive, out-of-control, berserker nation bearing no similarities whatsoever to the enlightened, God-anointed land where freedom and happiness reign.

S

SACRED, adj. In the United States, a synonym for "profitable." The related term "sacrosanct" normally means "highly profitable" or "already sold."

SADISTIC, adj. Popular, well thought of, a shoo-in for reelection.

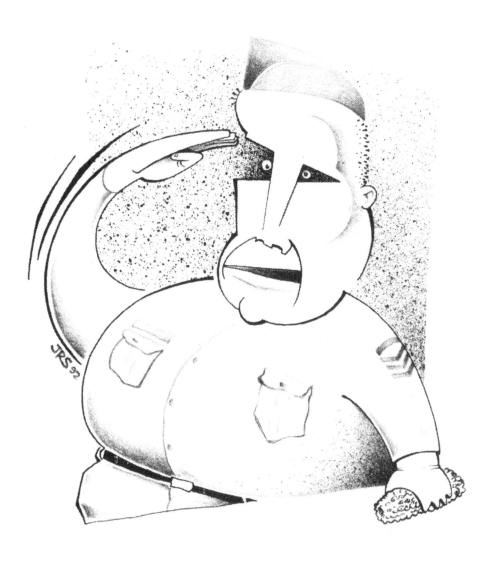

SALUTE, n. A ritualized military gesture of submission involving awkward arm and hand movements and a stiffening of the body similar to that produced by insertion of a corn cob. The salute was presumably adopted in deference to overweight military personnel who found it difficult to bend over, drop their pants, and grab their ankles.

SAFE, adj. A term employed by tobacco and chemical company "scientists" to describe products that they themselves would never, ever use.

SANCTIFY, v.t. 1) As Nietzsche points out, to denaturalize; 2) To designate non-"sanctified" things (especially portions of the Earth's surface) as fair game for despoliation.

SATYRIASIS, n. The preferred treatment regimen for nymphomania. (with a tip of the hat to the great, under-appreciated science fiction writer, John Brunner)

SCIENCE, n. A systematic means of understanding and describing the natural world. It is based on the scientific method. To simplify somewhat, that method consists of: 1) gathering as much data as possible on a phenomenon; 2) formulating a hypothesis to explain the data; 3) testing the hypothesis for internal consistency and to see if it is in accord with the data; 4) gathering additional data and seeing if the hypothesis is in accord with the additional data; and 5) checking whether predictions generated by the hypothesis are accurate.

Another way of putting this is that science is a systematic method of arriving at the most probably correct explanations of observed phenomena, given current knowledge.

An important adjunct to this is that science is fact driven rather than belief driven. So, scientists are bound to accept the results of scientific investigation even if they don't particularly like the results—if a pet theory is at odds with the facts, out goes the pet theory (eventually).

Thus science is the most powerful means ever devised of dispelling illusions. This is, of course, why it is almost universally despised in the United States.

SCUMBAG, n. See "Landlord."

SCUMBUCKET, n. See "Landlord."

SELF-ABUSE, n. A popular solitary activity usually involving the words "must" or "should." (with thanks to Albert Ellis)

SELF-MADE MAN, n. A businessman with a fortune of $10 million who began life under the handicap of inheriting a mere $1 million.

SELF-DELUSION, n. A practice which makes individual life tolerable and public life intolerable, given the tendency toward enshrinement of popular delusions in the penal code.

SELF-MORTIFICATION, n. (also known as "Mortification of the Flesh") The delight of the devout. The sensuality of the sanctified.

While, over the ages, many holy persons have indulged in self-mortification, St. Simeon Stylites is undoubtedly the model *par excellence* for saintly sybarites luxuriating in this earthly pleasure. In his *History of European Morals,* W.E.H. Lecky outlines St. Simeon's methods:

"[St. Simeon] had bound a rope around him so that it became embedded in his flesh, which putrefied around it. A horrible stench, intolerable to the bystanders, exhaled from his body, and worms dropped from him whenever he moved, and they filled his bed. . . .

"St. Simeon stood upon one leg, the other being covered with hideous ulcers, while his biographer [St. Anthony] was commissioned to stand by his side, to pick up the worms that fell from his body, and to replace them in the sores, the saint saying to the worms, 'Eat what God has given you.'"

One can assume that this holy man, indeed, this canonized saint, died a happy man.

SELF-PITY, n. A disgusting trait often needlessly exhibited by others, but never exhibited by oneself without good reason.

SELF-SACRIFICE, n. Arduous and admirable preparation for the more agreeable task of sacrificing others.

SENATOR, n. A millionaire or, if newly elected, about to become one.

SENSE OF WONDER, n. An attitude of awe, a quasi-religious sensation of sheer amazement, as upon discovering a narcotics agent or other "drug warrior" with respect for the Bill of Rights, individual liberties, and basic human decency.

SEQUEL, n. In the literary and cinematic fields, a betrayal of hope —proof that some people will do anything for money and that other people will pay money for anything.

SERVILE, adj. Docile. Readily employable.

SEX, n. According to a number of American women, a sequence of events which normally runs as follows: 1) Foreplay [consisting of the question, "Are you awake?"]; 2) Thirty to ninety seconds of grunting, pawing, fumbling, and other forms of ineptitude; 3) "That was great!"; 4) Snoring by one party; 5) Masturbation by the other. (with thanks to the anonymous woman who provided the definition of "Foreplay" on an e-mail list)

SHEEP, n. 1) A large, abysmally stupid quadruped bearing a striking resemblance to another common domesticated animal, the average American voter; 2) In many rural areas of the United States, a readily available surrogate for the Penthouse "Pet of the Month." It should be mentioned that the use to which the sheep is put under this definition is quite similar to that to which the average American voter is put by a predator known as the "average American politician." The difference lies in the fact that by entering the voting booth the average American voter voluntarily submits to the indignities visited upon him.

SINGLE, adj. Suffering impaired vision. When in public places, unable to see anything other than happy couples.

SITUATIONISM, n. A nihilistic French marxism variant epitomized by 600-page texts which were unreadable in the original and are unspeakable in translation. The basic assumption of situationism is that life today in the "Society of the Spectacle" is so "dominated" by "Capital" that organized resistance is useless and is "recuperated" in such a way as to strengthen said "Capital." Thus, the situation is hopeless and all attempts at social and political betterment are worse than useless. So, rather than waste their time on political activism, many situationists content themselves with wearing an all-black uniform, hanging around coffee houses, using French-marxist political jargon whenever possible, and sneering at those who do not share their insights. The more disturbed devote themselves to publishing ugly tabloid newspapers, the better to demonstrate the inferiority of those who disagree with them. Despite its waning appeal, this intellectually precocious form of despair is still reasonably popular in certain academic milieus where marxism alone is considered insufficiently pretentious.

SIZE, n. Matters. (according to a number of female friends)

SLAVERY, n. 1) Capitalism carried to its logical conclusion in the sphere of human relations; 2) A grossly immoral institution which flourished for 1,500 years in christian lands. In recent times, however, religious spokesmen have revealed that christianity was in the forefront of opposition to this great moral evil—just as religious spokesmen in coming ages will reveal that during the 20th and 21st centuries the Catholic Church led the fight to provide free contraception and abortion on demand in order to combat the evil of overpopulation.

SLEAZY, adj. A redundant term used for emphasis, as when placed before "politician," "lawyer," or "televangelist."

SMOKER, n. 1) A drug addict who believes that he has the right to annoy and poison those around him. Unlike the user of non-addictive drugs, the smoker is to be pitied and tolerated rather than spied upon, entrapped, and imprisoned. 2) A rugged, take-no-bullshit maverick who proudly shows his independence by flaunting his enslavement to the health-destroying products of multinational corporations.

SMOKERS' RIGHTS, n. pl. The sacred right of smokers to annoy others and to damage the health of nonsmokers in public places. While some do-good liberals might question this basic right, it should be noted that this is not an isolated right; smokers' rights are very much akin to another important individual liberty: "pissers' rights," the right to urinate on everyone in one's immediate vicinity.

SNAKE PIT, n. 1) A den of vipers; 2) A common euphemism for "academia."

SOCCER, n. An Un-American, foreign sport, very popular in Cuba, North Korea, Iran, and other dictatorships, mentioned in this dictionary only because certain persons insist upon referring to it as "football," a term properly reserved for an important American religious rite.

SOLDIER, n. A praiseworthy individual who practices the virtues of blindly obeying orders and of killing human beings whom he doesn't know (or, occasionally, those whom he does).

SPIRITUAL, adj. A term of self-congratulation used to assert superiority over others.

SPIRITUALITY, n. 1) A meaningless but uplifting term often found in "personals" ads; 2) As often encountered in the United States, a rank blend of arrogance, condescension, irrationality, and hypocrisy. Its more advanced practitioners refine this base amalgam to pure rhetoric uncontaminated by action, especially action beneficial to others.

STABLE, adj. A self-descriptive term often used in personals ads. Synonym: "on Prozac."

STOCK CAR RACING (more familiarly, "NASCAR") n. The unfortunate end product of generations of in-family dating and consumption of poisoned liquor in the southern United States.

STRUGGLE, n. 1) Physical exertion, such as that of a man single-handedly attempting to install a transmission in a 1964 Buick; 2) A nebulous but militant-sounding political term. When, at the close of a letter, it is preceded by the word "in," "struggle" can refer to any or, more often, no activity whatsoever. (thanks to the old transmission manhandler, Fred Woodworth, for the inspiration for this one)

STUPIDITY, n. An invaluable commodity. The grease which lubricates the wheels of American commerce, politics, and religion. Indeed, without a plentiful supply of this vital fluid, the American economic system would grind to a halt, Republicans would become an endangered species, and the televangelism industry would vanish into thin air—and not because it had become "unmanned" during the "rapture."

SUCCESS, n. As commonly conceived in the United States, the transformation of oneself from productive worker to parasite. The greater the degree of parasitism, the greater the degree of success. See also "Parasitology."

SUICIDE, n. Doing one's bit for the environment.

SUPERB, adj. An advertising term meaning substandard, average, or, in rare instances, a hair better than average.

SUPINE, adj. The customary position of journalists, especially noticeable at presidential press conferences and when avoiding investigative reporting. Synonym: "Fair and Balanced."

SUPPORT, v. Although still occasionally used as a transitive verb in its archaic sense of providing physical aid, the term now normally refers to the simple but sufficient act of affixing a bumper sticker to one's vehicle, most commonly one stating, "We Support Our Troops."

SURGICAL BOMBING, n. A devastating attack on civilian targets utilizing plentiful amounts of napalm and cluster bombs. See also "Collateral Damage" and "Regrettable Necessity."

SUSPENDERS, n. For women, see "Warning Signs." Synonyms: "Mustache," "Muttonchops," "Motorcycle." The corresponding tip-offs for men include varnished-on makeup, names such as "Windspirit" and "Summerstorm," refusal to use the standard spelling of "women," and "Don't worry, I'll be divorced soon" (also phrased, "Don't worry, the relationship is really over"). (with thanks to Brian Hullfish and Randy Oliver for the final two warning signs)

T

TATTOO, n. A common, nonverbal means of saying "Look at me! Look at me!" while avoiding the tedious work so necessary to real distinction. Synonyms: "Branding," "Scarification," "Body Piercing."

TAX, n. A voluntary contribution to the government. Those making such contributions are, of course, happy to donate several months of their annual income to the state, resting confident in the knowledge that their public servants will spend their money in wiser, more beneficent ways than they themselves, individually or collectively, could ever hope to devise.

TELEVANGELIST, n. Ideally suited to his profession, the televangelist makes a career of denouncing greed, gluttony, dishonesty, drunkenness, drug abuse, prostitution, adultery, fornication, and homosexuality—and thus speaks from a wealth of personal experience.

TELEPHONE, n. A communications device activated by pressure on the seat of a commode.

TEMPORARY, adj. Permanent. As in "temporary tax increase" and "temporary price increase." (with apologies to a science fiction writer [Heinlein?] who pointed this out decades ago)

TEN COMMANDMENTS, n. pl. The fundamental moral precepts of the christian and jewish faiths, and a fine set of guiding lights for us all. Some low-minded skeptics have suggested that god could have improved upon these inspired moral principles if it had dropped the commandments concerning swearing, idol worship, sexual exclusivity, and resting on the sabbath, and had instead instituted bans on slavery, torture, and cruelty; but these suggestions are obviously ill advised and sacrilegious. If slavery, torture, and cruelty were true moral evils, organized christianity would not have condoned, instigated, and practiced all three for the better part of two millennia. Fortunately, most christians realize this and do not bother themselves about trifles such as cruelty, torture, and economic exploitation. Instead, they rightly concentrate their moral outrage on the true evils of "obscene" books and pictures, "filthy" language, and the sexual practices of their neighbors.

TERM LIMITS, n. A reform intended to benefit the republic by limiting the number of terms elected officials may serve, thus affording a wider range of individuals the opportunity to do harm.

TERROR, n. Extreme fear—an exceptionally unpleasant emotion which produces physical symptoms such as a pounding heart, clenched jaw, sweaty palms, and, occasionally, brown trousers. This disturbing emotion is most commonly triggered in American males, in its most gut-wrenching form, by the words, "Honey, we need to talk."

TERRORISM, n. The threat or use of deadly force by callous, hardened egomaniacs for the purpose of intimidating others into bending to their dictates. The term does not, of course, refer to the benevolent activities of the police and military. And, needless to say, the term should never be applied to the economic conditions and policies that inspire countless Americans to hang on for dear life to jobs that they loathe.

TERRORIST, n. One who uses violence in a manner contrary to the interests of U.S.-based multinational corporations. Thus, Saddam Hussein was not a terrorist (and in fact received billions of dollars of U.S. "aid") while he was slaughtering thousands of Kurdish civilians with nerve gas during the 1980s, but instantly became "another Hitler" when he threatened U.S. oil interests in Kuwait; and Osama Bin Laden was a "freedom fighter," not a terrorist, during the 1980s when he was fighting the Soviets in Afghanistan and receiving CIA-delivered U.S. "aid."

TERRORIST THREAT, n. (also "Terrorist State") Any country with large oil reserves not under U.S. control. Not to be confused with harmless U.S. allies employing death squads or developing nuclear weapons.

TEXAS, n. The state: 1) where men are still men and women will do if sheep aren't available; 2) where the opposable thumb is considered a new and dangerously radical innovation; 3) where the winner of the state beauty pageant is usually named "Bubba" (which largely explains definition #1); and 4) which is a nice place, if it weren't for the Texans. (with a tip of the ten-gallon hat to Earl Lee, who knows whereof he speaks)

THEOLOGY, n. Imagination raised to a "science."

THIEF, n. One who wrongfully obtains the property of others, but is so unwise as to do it on a small scale.

TO PROTECT AND SERVE, phr. The motto of those who break strikes, harass gay, black and hispanic people, spy upon political activists, brutally suppress public demonstrations of free speech, bust people for smoking pot and for other victimless "crimes," are virtually powerless to prevent violent crimes such as rape and murder, and who often won't even bother to investigate such minor matters as home burglaries and auto break-ins. See also "Perjury," "Resisting Arrest," and "Assaulting an Officer."

Tobacco, n. A toxic, addictive substance, the chief drawback of which is that it doesn't kill its users more quickly.

Tongue, n. A fleshy organ rooted to the floor of the mouth, useful in oral sex and the polishing of boot leather.

Tough, adj. A term used by admiring journalists to describe powerful politicians, especially the U.S. president and other heads of state. It normally means: 1) callous; 2) having little regard for human life; 3) ready and willing to shed the blood of others while running no personal risk of injury.

Traditional Values, n. pl. The bedrock of the nation: fear of the unknown; hatred of the unorthodox; anti-intellectualism; racism; sexism; homophobia; sexual repression; fear and loathing of the human body; the morbid prurience of the "moral"; enjoyment of the sadistic infliction of pain; an ignorance-is-strength, faith-not-reason philosophy; a preference for "faith" over facts; blind belief in the tyranny of the majority; censorship; gullibility; mindless support of the government, especially in time of war; rejoicing over slaughter; a sheep-like longing for "strong leaders"; the desire to make a buck at any price to the environment or to other people; toadying behavior toward one's bosses; bullying behavior toward one's subordinates; intolerance of anyone who deviates one scintilla from a narrow, christian "morality"; the desire to inflict pain on the "immoral"; and the desire to force them to be "moral" through the use of violence, coercion, torture, imprisonment, and execution. Without these Traditional Values, America would not be what it is today.

Traditionalist, n. One who desires the continuance of dangerous, vicious, and unethical practices because they have already done so much harm.

Trailer, n. (also "Mobile Home") The preferred abode of Midwestern and Southern thrill seekers. Synonym: "Tornado Magnet."

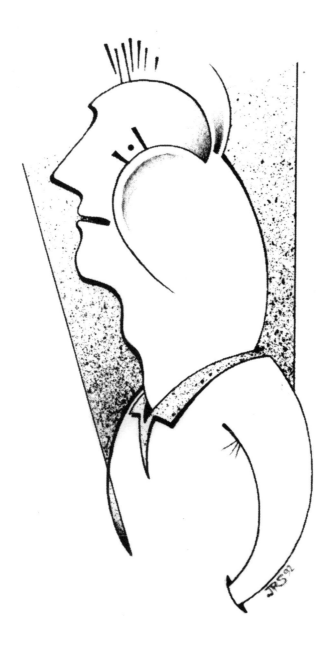

TRUTHFUL, adj. Unappreciated, unloved, and unemployed.

TROTSKYISM, n. Stalinism deprived of state power. (with apologies to an anarchist who pointed this out years ago in, I believe, *Freedom Fortnightly*, and whose name I've long since forgotten)

TROTSKYISTS, n. pl. Adherents to one of the 57 varieties of leninism, trotskyists are uniquely reluctant to bury the hatchet with their stalinist foes. Few in number, though fractious, one trotskyist constitutes a "split"; two constitute a "group"; three constitute a "movement"; and four constitute an "International" (especially if one of the four lives in a different city than the others).

TRUE, adj. A term of approval used to describe anything in which one wishes to believe, as in the common phrase, "The True Faith."

TRUST, n. 1) An emotion or attitude, mostly misplaced, as in, "Trust me. I know what I'm doing." 2) In religion, commerce, and politics, a term which is incomplete unless preceded by the words "abuse of" or "betrayal of."

TYRANNY OF THE MAJORITY, n. See "United States of America."

U

UFO, n. An acronym commonly believed to stand for Unidentified Flying Object, but in fact standing for Uncommonly Foolish Observer. The term is invariably used in this sense in press reports of "UFO sightings."

UNAMERICAN, n. A term of the highest praise, often used, paradoxically, as if it had a derogatory meaning.

UNBIASED REPORTING, ger. The shoring up of the political and economic status quo through journalistic means. These include the publishing or broadcasting of government and corporate press releases as "news"; the publishing or broadcasting of the remarks of government officials without comment, even when Unbiased Reporters know the remarks to be untrue (pointing out that such remarks are "misstatements" is a sure sign of "bias"); and careful avoidance of asking such valued "sources" anything approaching an embarrassing question. If Unbiased Reporters carefully follow these "fair and balanced" practices, they can be reasonably assured of continual and lucrative employment, the esteem of their colleagues, and a plentiful supply of government and corporate posteriors in which to affix their nasal passages.

UNEMPLOYMENT, n. Escape from the shackles of a dull, soul-destroying job into the manacles of economic desperation.

UNITARIAN, n. An atheist unable to kick the habit of self-abasement.

UNITED STATES OF AMERICA, n. The land of the fee and the home of the slave. (John Rush's fine definition, which needs no further elaboration)

UNIVERSITY, n. In the United States, an institution uncompromisingly committed to the pursuit of excellence in football and, occasionally, other academic disciplines (most commonly basketball).

U.S. MILITARY, n. 1) A vital institution which wisely utilizes resources which might otherwise be wasted on food, housing, education, and medicine; 2) The U.S. government's last line of defense against the menace of freedom, both at home and abroad.

UTOPIAN, adj. A pejorative term meaning neither in the interests of the powers that be nor of those who would like to take their places.

V

VAMPIRE, n. The world over, from Boro Boro to the Borgo Pass, an owner of rental properties.

VEGETARIANISM, n. Squeamishness tinged with self-righteousness. (with thanks to Bill Griffith, one of whose *Griffith Observatory* strips inspired this definition)

VERBAL AGREEMENT, n. A legally binding contract worth the full value of the paper upon which it is written. (yet another chestnut from the famous wit, Anonymous)

VERTICALLY CHALLENGED, adj. In this enlightened age, the only proper term with which to describe a four-foot-tall adult. Synonym: "Differently Statured."

VETERAN, n. A person who increased the power of the government by killing human beings opposed to it, and who now expects victims of governmental extortion to reward him in perpetuity.

VICIOUS, adj. Popular, electable, having a reputation for moral rectitude.

VITAL AMERICAN INTERESTS, n. pl. An inspiring reason to lay down one's life in battle. Synonym: "Oil."

VOTING, ger. The opportunity to inflict pain and suffering upon others through the election of politicians wielding coercive power, or, more gratifyingly, directly through the initiative process.

Vulgar, adj. In regard to literary and musical works, popular, profitable, and highly regarded.

Wage Labor, n. 1) Death on the installment plan; 2) The process by which those who work enrich those who don't.

Wallet, n. The more important of the two male sexual organs —the larger the wallet, the more attractive the male. Individuals of the opposite sex, more often than not, are referring to this organ when they coo, "Oooh honey, you have such a big one!"

War, n. A time-tested political tactic guaranteed to raise an incumbent president's popularity rating by at least 30 points. It is especially useful during election years and economic downturns.

Warranty, n. A convenient device for gauging the useful lifetime of a product, that lifetime normally being one day longer than the lifetime of the warranty, though in extreme cases it can be up to a full month longer.

Washed in the Blood, adj. phrase. As considered by fundamentalists, the ideal state of personal hygiene.

WE, pron. 1) The smallest but most useful tool in the political demagogue's bag of verbal tricks. Even more than the exceedingly useful "our," "we" is indispensable in making it appear that individuals who have very little in common—such as the rich and those who do useful work—have similar or identical interests; 2) A term frequently found in the discourse of morons when they attempt to discuss political and economic issues. Interestingly, the statements in which mental defectives use this propaganda term are often identical to those in which political manipulators use the term (though the motivations of the two groups are very different), as in "We should all pull together and support our troops."

WEASEL, n. A small, ferret-like animal often found practicing corporate law or conducting White House press conferences.

WEATHER, n. A very safe, hence perennially popular, topic of conversation among slaves. (with apologies to a writer, whose name I've forgotten, who pointed this out ages ago in, I believe, *Processed World*)

WHIP, v. To motivate forcefully—always, of course, reluctantly and for the victim's own good, often to assist him in the removal of some moral defect to which he is blind, but which is most apparent to the keener vision of his well-wishers. See also "Regrettable Necessity."

WHIP, n. A means of motivation formerly much used by employers (in some places unkindly called "slave owners"). In our more enlightened age, the whip has been largely displaced by the more humane means of motivation of unemployment, hunger, and homelessness, wielded by benefactors known as "investors," "entrepreneurs," and "job creators." (with apologies to Bierce)

WHITE SKIN PRIVILEGE, n. Code words through which politically correct whites recognize each other. The term is especially useful in that it has the potential to induce guilt in even the poorest and most exploited caucasians.

WHITE SUPERIORITY, n. The fond dream of those whose existence is the strongest evidence against it.

WOMEN'S MUSIC, n. American folk music with "new age" over-tones, stripped of what little musical interest folk music normally possesses, and marked by occasional acts of musical desecration, such as that of a fourth-rate flautist attempting to solo over the first movement of Beethoven's "Moonlight Sonata." While this lexicographer would never question the prescience of those who coined the term "Women's Music," he still wonders on occasion if the women of Zimbabwe, for instance, listen to and perform this sub-genre of American folk music.

WISHFUL THINKING, ger. 1) A popular form of spirituality often referred to as "Faith" or "Belief," though "Hope" seems more appropriate; 2) The practice of those who find their existences intolerable and have no confidence in their abilities to improve their own lives. The more extravagant their wishful thinking, and the more desperately they cling to it, the "deeper" such persons consider their "faith," and the "sorrier" they are for those lacking the "ability" to share that "faith."

WITCH, n. To fundamentalist christians, a burning curiosity—and a curiosity which many of them, even at this late date, hope to reignite.

WOMYN, n. Also "Wimmin," "Wimin," "Womin," "Wymyn," "Wymmyn," "Wommyn," and even, occasionally, "Women." An indication of the success achieved by the U.S. educational system in fostering diversity in spelling and grammar. See also "Speling Be" and "Litterusy."

WORK, n. The curse of the drinking class. (according to Oscar Wilde)

WORKING POOR, n. A term so common as to pass by virtually unnoticed, but perhaps the ultimate comment on the gratifying fairness of the Free Enterprise System—a system in which those who do the most fundamentally necessary, frequently unpleasant work are often rewarded with poverty. To fully savor this delectable if familiar term, try to pronounce its near relative, "the working rich," without smiling.

WRISTWATCH, n. A type of slave bracelet, useful in prodding the slave to appear when others wish him to.

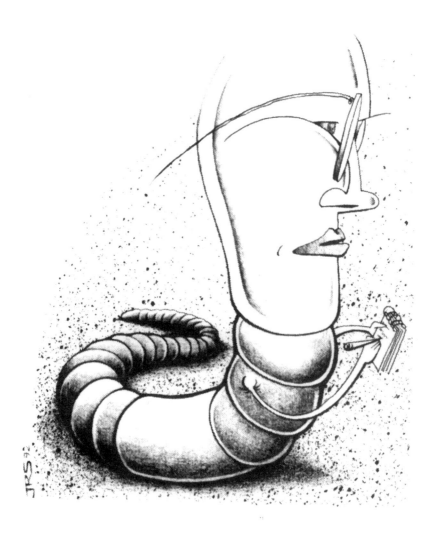

Worms, n. pl. Soft-bodied invertebrates which lie prostrate and propel themselves by crawling on their bellies, much in the manner of the White House press corps.

X-ACTO, n. A beautifully designed, extremely useful graphic arts tool utilizing a razor-sharp cutting edge ideally suited to reminding novice graphic artists, through loss of blood, that they are in fact novices.

Now, sad to say, this is rapidly becoming an archaic definition thanks to computers. Decades ago, Frank Zappa opined that, "It's too bad that stupidity isn't painful." Until recently—and almost uniquely—thanks to the X-acto, at least some forms of stupidity *were* painful.

XENOPHOBIA, n. An intense hatred of foreigners and things foreign, and a corresponding strong preference for one's countrymen and things domestic. Hence, in the United States, a form of dementia.

YELLOW RIBBON, n. As displayed in public, a symbolic representation of a human tongue gliding softly and carressingly over boot leather—as featured in the innumerable "Welcome Home Desert Stormtroopers" festivities celebrating the mass slaughter of near-helpless Iraqi conscripts in full retreat during the first Gulf War and the return home of the slaughterers.

YES DEAR, excl. For women, an indication that the speaker is not listening to them. Synonyms: "Yes, honey," "Of course, honey," "Anything you say, dear."

YOUTH, n. A novice in the art of misspending one's life.

YOUTH-ORIENTED, adj. phr. A movie-advertising term meaning: 1) Shallow, insipid, and an insult to any youth with an IQ over 80; 2) In desperate need of the leavening ingredients of experience and cynicism. Synonym: "Box Office Smash."

Z

ZEUS, n. 1) At the risk of redundancy, a mythological deity; 2) Like the entries beginning with "K," "Q," and "X," a term included in this dictionary because of the compulsive tendencies of a lexicographer who shall remain nameless.

Some Relevant Quotations

The following quotations amplify or illustrate points made in the preceding definitions. All of them are taken from *The Heretic's Handbook of Quotations (Second Edition)*, Charles Bufe, editor.

Mikhail Bakunin

People go to church for the same reasons they go to a tavern: to stupefy themselves, to forget their misery, to imagine themselves, for a few minutes anyway, free and happy.

—*A Circular Letter to My Friends in Italy*

William Blake

Prisons are built with stones of law, brothels with bricks of religion.

—*Proverbs of Hell*

Henry Thomas Buckle

. . . the United States of America, that wretched burlesque of an ancient republic which possesses the forms of democracy without the spirit of liberty.

—*The Causes and Effects of Duelling*

Al Capone

This American system of ours, call it Americanism, call it capitalism, call it what you like, gives each and every one of us a great opportunity if we only seize it with both hands and make the most of it.

Samuel Taylor Coleridge

He saw a lawyer killing a viper
    On a dunghill hard by his own stable;
And the Devil smiled, for it put him in mind
    Of Cain and his Brother Abel.

—*The Devil's Thoughts*

Stephen Crane

These stupid peasants, who, throughout the world, hold potentates on their thrones, make statesmen illustrious, provide generals with lasting victories, all with ignorance, indifference, or half-witted hatred, moving the world with the strength of their arms, and getting their heads knocked together in the name of God, the king, or the stock exchange —immortal, dreaming, hopeless asses, who surrender their reason to the care of a shining puppet, and persuade some toy to carry their lives in his purse.

—quoted by Jack London in *People of the Abyss*

Clarence Darrow

I don't believe in God, because I don't believe in Mother Goose.

Ralph Waldo Emerson

Nothing is more disgusting than the crowing about liberty by slaves, as most men are, and the flippant mistaking for freedom of some paper preamble like a Declaration of Independence or the statute right to vote . . . .

—*The Conduct of Life*

Anatole France

The law, in its majestic equality, forbids the rich as well as the poor to sleep under bridges, to beg in the streets, and to steal bread.

Edward Gibbon

The various modes of worship which prevailed in the Roman world were all considered by the people as equally true; by the philosopher as equally false; and by the magistrate as equally useful.

—*The Decline and Fall of the Roman Empire*

Emma Goldman

That the mass bleeds, that it is being robbed and exploited, I know as well as our vote-baiters. But I insist that not the handful of parasites, but the mass itself is responsible for this horrible state of affairs. It clings to its masters, loves the whip, and is the first to cry Crucify! the moment a protesting voice is raised against the sacredness of capitalistic authority or any other decayed institution. Yet how long would authority and private property exist, if not for the willingness of the mass to become soldiers, policemen, jailers, and hangmen?

—*Francisco Ferrer and the Modern School*

Reggie Jackson

For the right amount amount of money, you're willing to eat Alpo.

—quoted in *The Sporting News*, February 1, 1988

Peter Kropotkin

America is just the country that shows how all the written guarantees in the world for freedom are no protection against tyranny and oppression of the worst kind.

Errico Malatesta

The only possible alternative to being either the oppressed or the oppressor is voluntary cooperation for the good of all.

—*Volonta*, June 15, 1913

Johann Most

Not man as such, but man in connection with wealth is a beast of prey. The richer a man, the greater his need for more. We may call such a man "the beast of property." . . . It is the lash of hunger which compels the poor man to submit. In order to live he must sell—"voluntarily" sell—himself every day and hour to the "beast of property."

—*The Beast of Property*

Friedrich Nietzsche

Belief means *not wanting* to know what is true.

"Salvation of the soul"—in plain words, the world revolves around *me*."

Belief removes no mountains, but places mountains where there are none. A hasty walk through a madhouse enlightens sufficiently on these matters. Not to a priest to be sure: for he denies by instinct that sickness is sickness and a madhouse is a madhouse.

That little hypocrites and half-crazed people dare to imagine that on their account the laws of nature are constantly *broken*—such an enhancement of every kind of selfishness to infinity, to *impudence,* cannot be branded with sufficient contempt. And yet Christianity owes its *triumph* to this pitiable flattery of personal vanity.

One is not converted to Christianity, one must be morbid enough for it.

—above Nietzsche quotations from *The Anti-Christ*

Wendell Phillips

The liberties of the freest people are in danger when they set up symbols of liberty as fetishes, worshiping the symbol instead of the principle it represents.

Pierre Joseph Proudhon

Laws: We know what they are and what they are worth! They are spider webs for the rich and mighty, steel chains for the poor and weak, fishing nets in the hands of the government.

Arthur Schopenhauer

Princes use God as a kind of bogey with which to frighten grown-up children into bed, if nothing else avails; that's why they attach so much importance to the deity.

—*Religion, A Dialogue*

Hiram Stafford

Individual possession is the great entering wedge, which has split society into eight hundred million fragments . . . It virtually, practically, and theoretically denies the brotherhood of man.

—*The Liberator*, September 8, 1844

George Steinbrenner

I think we could put Adolf Hitler in center field and fans would cheer for him if he hit .350.

—quoted in *The Sporting News*, March 13, 1989

Max Stirner

The great are great only because we are on our knees. Let us rise!

—*The Ego and His Own*

Allen Thornton

What do you think "govern" means? It doesn't mean "suggest" or "implore." It doesn't mean two people sitting down, talking it over and compromising. "Govern" means "force," and "force" means "violence." . . . Laws are merely whims backed up with guns, and taxes are simply the extortionist's requests for money. Isn't it natural, then, that governments are often led by immoral men? . . . One day the very idea of government will seem like an insane artifact of the past [like] witch burning, crusading, black slavery, prohibition.

—*Laws of the Jungle*

John Wycliffe

Lords devour poor men's goods in gluttony and waste and pride, and they perish for mischief and thirst and cold, and their children also . . . And so in a manner they eat and drink poor men's flesh and blood.

Emile Zola

Civilization will not attain to its perfection until the last stone from the last church falls on the last priest.

Other See Sharp Press Titles

If you enjoyed *The Devil's Dictionaries*, you'll probably also enjoy:

The Heretic's Handbook of Quotations (Second Edition), Charles Bufe, editor. More than 2000 quotations on politics, sex, religion, and over 20 other topics. Includes dozens of illustrations. $16.95 / 238 pp. (7"x10") / ISBN 1-884365-27-2

The Philosophy of Friedrich Nietzsche, by H.L. Mencken. Mencken's clear, very entertaining introduction to Nietzsche. This See Sharp Press edition contains many new explanatory notes and a new introduction by Charles Bufe. $9.95 / 178 pp. (6"x9") / ISBN 1-884365-31-0

The Anti-Christ, by Friedrich Nietzsche. Nietzsche's final book—a succinct, biting indictment of Christianity. This edition contains a lengthy introduction by its translator, H.L. Mencken. $6.95 / 91 pp. / ISBN 1-884365-20-5

(Additional copies of **The Devil's Dictionaries** are, of course, available for $9.95.)

For a single book, please add $3 P/H. For two books, there is no P/H fee. If you order three, there is no P/H fee and you'll receive a free copy of priest-turned-atheist Joseph McCabe's pamphlet, *How Christianity Grew Out of Paganism*. And if you order all four books, there is no P/H fee and you'll receive both *How Christianity Grew Out of Paganism* and another McCabe pamphlet, *Pagan Christs*.

Please send me the following: _____

_____

Print Name _____ **Address** _____

City _____ **State** _____ **Zip** _____

Please send check or money order to **See Sharp Press, P.O. Box 1731, Tucson, AZ 85702-1731**.

Our full catalog is available on line at www.seesharppress.com